TRUE

HEART

A WAY TO SELFLESSNESS

WILLIAM M. WATSON, SJ

OTHER BOOKS BY WILLIAM M. WATSON, SJ

Sacred Story:
An Ignatian Examen for the Third Millennium

Inviting God into Your Life:
A Practical Guide for Prayer

FORTY WEEKS:
An Ignatian Path to Christ with Sacred Story Prayer

Reflections and Homilies:
The Gonzaga Collection

Sacred Story Rosary:
An Ignatian Way to Pray the Mysteries

Sacred Story Affirmations

The Whole-Life Confession

My Sacred Story Missal

Understanding the Spiritual World

Forty Weeks ~ Letters From Prison

Forty Weeks ~ A Journey of Healing and Transformation for Priests

Sacred Story Press
1401 E Jefferson St, STE 405
Seattle, WA 98122

Dedicated the Sacred Heart & Immaculate Heart

IMPRIMI POTEST
Scott R. Santarosa, S.J.
IMPRIMATUR
George V. Murry, SJ
Bishop of Youngstown

Unless otherwise indicated, Scripture quotations are from the Holy Bible, New American Bible, revised edition © 2010, 1991, 1986, 1970 Confraternity of Christian Doctrine, Washington, D.C.

Cover and Book Design: William Watson, SJ *Holy Wings*: I choose the image of wings to evoke the freedom that living your TRUE HEART will bring to you. (All other art images are in the public domain or have been allowed use by designating authorship. If you believe otherwise, contact: admin-team@sacredstory.net)

Manufactured in the United States of America
ISBN- 9781986564250

THE POWER OF TRUE HEART

Discerning a priestly vocation is not a matter of learning a craft, but of allowing the grace of God to transform our heart after Christ's own Heart. like St. Ignatius did. Despite their great desires., young men today have difficulty understanding how to do that. In a culture saturated with noise and distraction, it is harder than ever to sift through the competing voices to hear the voice of the Father and to respond virtuously and courageously.

TRUE HEART adapts the timeless method of St. Ignatius to our own day and time. Using this program, young men and women can encounter the Risen Lord and respond to Him in a profoundly personal way in the Sacraments, prayer, and lives of virtue. Seminarians and those discerning the seminary will find that the TRUE HEART exercises and other material are useful resources in leading them to a deep daily encounter with Jesus. From this place of encounter, they will be better able to hear the Lord's call and respond as Mary did.

-Very Rev. Daniel J. Barnett – Rector
Bishop White Seminary – Spokane, WA

The Spiritual Exercises of St. Ignatius of Loyola are one of the great spiritual treasures in the Church. Ignatian spirituality has formed countless saints and holy men and women over the past five centuries. We are indebted to Fr. Bill Watson for making this spiritual treasure accessible to a new generation. It is certain to bear much fruit for many years into the future.

-Steve Bollman
Founder & President – Paradisus Dei
Author – "That Man Is You" – "The Choice Wine"

In speaking with university students and listening to their concerns, certain areas always enter into the conversation. "How do I Pray?", "How can I know what God's wants me to do?", "How do I learn more about discernment?" These are areas that young adults question constantly because they have a desire to grow in holiness and faith. TRUE HEART is a very approachable program that addresses these issues and more.

I cannot wait to challenge the students and implement TRUE HEART as a semester long program at Rice University. It is set up as a turn-key program that can be led by campus ministers, chaplains or student leaders. It can also be implemented within small group communities of men, women or co-ed. I am excited for our Catholic Students to experience TRUE HEART so they, in turn, can experience the true love that God has for His children.

-Rev. Ray Cook, OMI
Director of Campus Ministry – Rice University – Houston, TX

In TRUE HEART, Fr. Bill Watson has created a truly unique toolkit for youth and young adult formation. I could write countless endorsements about countless aspects of the TRUE HEART program that are noteworthy, and the reader might be led to think, Davidson just wants to praise everything. SO not true. I am very critical of these types of resources, having created many, and utilized many, I know too well the myriad ways they often fall short of what is needed for formation.

TRUE HEART is simply extraordinary. I personally am so excited to have these for use with my Confirmation classes and in many other formation settings. I am grateful I am for Fr. Bill Watson's diligent and extraordinary work. I stand in awe of what Fr. Bill Watson produced—the breadth and depth blow my mind.

For those seeking a program, TRUE HEART provides a detailed, user-friendly, comprehensive curriculum. For those seeking more flexible learning modules and experiences, TRUE HEART gives you an extraordinary toolkit that can be flexibly adapted and seamlessly integrated to supplement other programs, or for use in every kind of retreat or formation experience. I have used knowledge and tools from TRUE HEART with middle school, high school, college, and young adult settings. TRUE HEART not only provides essential knowledge about the faith; it is the perfect balance of deep content and flexible implementation needed to create an authentic and engaging experience of the faith. I cannot recommend it more highly!

-Matt Davidson, Ph.D.

President, Institute for Excellence & Ethics (IEE)

The Sacred Story Institute is at the leading edge of wisdom development in both children and adults. Now the Institute and its founder, Fr. William Watson, have created a very powerful set of programs for youth and young adults called TRUE HEART. These programs--one for individual young adults and one for youth and young adult leaders--help those who use them to remain grounded in real life, discover the beauty of existence at elemental levels, face the challenges young adults face in a high-pressure world, and protect their spiritual and emotional development from digital distress. I highly recommend the TRUE HEART programs.

-Michael Gurian

New York Times bestselling author

The Wonder of Boys and *The Minds of Girls*

In my years of work with high school students in retreat settings and teaching meditation classes, I find that the TRUE HEART resources are comprehensive and foundational for young adults to building stronger, long-lasting experiences in the Lord as they seek purposeful direction in their lives as they are called to building the Kingdom of God. The spirituality program Fr. Bill Watson, SJ offers in TRUE HEART: A Way to Selflessness, invites young adults to create, sustain and live out a deeper relationship with Jesus Christ using the spiritual practices of St. Ignatius Loyola but with a modern twist.

Young adults will encounter the Lord through time-proven spiritual methods such as:

✠ Unplugging intentionally from technology (distractions) during periods of time daily to remain open to the spiritual sphere of life

✠ Daily prayer periods that are rooted in the Ignatian Examen

✠ Spiritual exercises that point out roadblocks to living freely the spiritual life

✠ Young adults interacting and sharing with other young adult prayer companions

✠ Experiencing night vigils modeled on the Ignatian Spiritual Exercises

✠ Engaging with trusted mentors who can guide with wisdom, experience and faith

This time of communion with God peels away the false self of the young adult, as a companion of Jesus, and feeds their authentic self that leads to spiritual maturation.

-Andrew K. Hoelperl

Theology Department Chair – McQuaid Jesuit – Rochester, NY

True Heart Practices provides a practical Ignatian roadmap that will help young people speak, heart to heart, with our Living God. As Pope Francis continues to remind us that Christ Lives (Christus Vivit), this resource helps the reader practice the art of meditation in a vivid and relatable way.

-Jonathan Lewis

Assistant Secretary for Pastoral Ministry and Social Concerns

Archdiocese of Washington

The "'TRUE HEART' program offers resources for young adults and their formation leaders that provide simple and practical introductions to Ignatian prayer that will help all who use them to discover the deepest desire of their hearts: 'selflessness" and a daily living relationship with Jesus Christ. "

-Curtis Martin

Founder & CEO of FOCUS (Fellowship of Catholic University Students)

It is not true that young adults are not interested in religion as such. Young adults are not interested in a Christianity which, in their perception, is completely irrelevant to who they are. What if we told them that it is precisely Christ they need to understand their truest heart? TRUE HEART does this and much more! Fr. Watson's program not only awakens a passionate longing for authenticity, it actually takes you step by step, with the wise pedagogy of St. Ignatius and his sons, away from self-centeredness towards pure, selfless freedom.

My college students often ask, OK, I want to do this "Jesus thing" but what does it really mean in practice? How do you become that person God made you to be? TRUE HEART gives young people a perfect answer to this very question. I am excited for the new opportunities campus ministries around the country receive in Fr. Watson's TRUE HEART, and I wish I had had TRUE HEART 'S wonderful toolkit earlier!

-Fr. Lukasz Misko, OP

Director – St. Catherine of Siena Newman Center – the University of Utah – Salt Lake City, UT & President/Director – Dominican Liturgical Center Foundation – Krakow, Poland

*In the past God spoke to our ancestors through the prophets at many times and in various ways, but in these last days he has spoken to us by his Son... (Hebrews 1, 1-2a) " This is the core of TRUE HEART that the **Sacred Story Institute** has given us for our work with youth and young adults. TRUE HEART is a real effort to make the Word of God as near as it can be, for the new generations that hunger and thirst of an intimate encounter with their Creator.*

There are no magical tricks to change our lives, but the daring invitation to make fascinating treks to build a new way with the solid truths of what God has revealed to us in his Son. The TRUE HEART programs constantly focus on the chief cornerstone, and hold fast to it, giving it a new language so it can be better heard and understood by a new generation.

-Rev. Hermann Rodríguez Osorio, S.J.

Delegate for Mission

Jesuit Provincial's Conference of Latin America (CPAL)

I have been privileged to work with Fr. Watson, S.J. for several years during the development of the TRUE HEART program. This life-changing guide is the culmination of years of research and study, both scholarly and with actual teen and young adult groups, in schools and parishes nationwide and in Latin America. What gives TRUE HEART its depth and breathe is the up-to-date scientific research and day to day experiences associated with adolescents and young adults in the 21st century. TRUE HEART offers daily periods of reflection tightly woven with Scripture study leading to the desire to reach out to others from the students own awakening and new awareness.

Fr. Bill's profound and graced experiences of Sacred Story and now TRUE HEART for adolescents and young adults connect the modern trend of mindfulness practice with the ancient practice of lecio divena that has engaged my students precisely where they are and humbly sharing with them the gateway to the God of Jesus of Nazareth and the Risen Christ. TRUE HEART exceeds one's expectations of an "all-in-one" program. It does so simply because the TRUE HEART experience provides the door through which each individual may discover God in themselves—and others—in the present moment. I cannot say the same of any other program I've tried in a thirty-plus year career in Catholic education.

I highly recommend this program for yourself and also to share with youth groups, secondary Theology Classes, school student unions working toward tolerance and equality, Newman Centers and young adult parish programs and other groups of young people searching for God now.

-Marcella M. Nesbitt

Theology Instructor — McQuaid Jesuit — Rochester, NY

As an educator, I am so grateful to have a resource like TRUE HEART This program will help students balance the connectivity they find through their devices with a deeper connection to what is going on in their hearts. TRUE HEART will help young people discover a loving God who wants to walk alongside of them in the exciting and difficult journey of adolescence. I cannot wait to have my students benefit from this program.

-Jose Oyanguren

Headmaster – St. Augustine Prep – Managua, Nicaragua

TRUE HEART is a dynamic, prayerful, and timely resource for young adults to engage more deeply in a relationship with Jesus Christ. The 10-weeks of intentional prayer, quiet, and spiritual discipline will serve to open their minds and hearts to hear more clearly the ways God is speaking to them and calling them deeper. Fr. Bill says it best in the foreword- if 2% of people answer the call to participate in TRUE HEART, the other 98% will be deeply impacted by the overflow of love and devotion to Christ they develop.

I appreciate the Leader Resource Guide, as well, and would highly recommend this to leaders of young adult groups as they plan days of reflections, retreats, and other programs. Prayer is the most important way to maintain a relationship with God, and TRUE HEART offers a training regimen to instill a habit of prayer and listening to God that will be life-changing for young adults! God bless you in using TRUE HEART,

-Megan Pepin

Director of Young Adult Ministry — Archdiocese of Seattle

TRUE HEART is a brilliant pioneering effort from Fr. Bill Watson. He masterfully plays spiritual matchmaker with our youth and young adults today and invites them into the resplendent vision of St. Ignatius of Loyola's timeless wisdom for human flourishing.

Fr. Watson opens the deep beauty of Ignatian practice and mindfully offers us a guided tour on how to apply its powerful relevance as a balance to our modern digital lives. Fr. Watson's work here is a profound opportunity for youth and young adults to directly encounter the footsteps of Ignatius who leads us to the heart of Jesus Christ.

The youth and young adults we share TRUE HEART with will encounter Christ's grace in personal and transformative ways they never knew were possible. To revisit the steps of Fr. Watson's process from the initial meetings with my students at O'Dea to this final stage is truly awesome.

-**Tom Schutte**
Theology Educator – O'Dea High School – Seattle, WA

The TRUE HEART program is a unique opportunity for young people to undergo Spiritual Exercises within their busy everyday life. Fr William skillfully adapts his wonderful Sacred Story methodologies to the needs of busy students. He is very aware of the challenges young people face and so places emphasis on topics like the use of technology and the struggle with self-respect.

TRUE HEART program helps to understand and deepen the experience of the sacrament of Reconciliation. It provides a great introduction to reading and meditating the Scripture.

The whole program is so constructed that it is accessible for both those who just start an intentional faith life as well as for those who want to deepen their existing relationship with God. I wholeheartedly recommend this program for Youth and

Young Adult leadership teams. I also recommend it for young adults wishing to grow in their faith who also want to discern life choices in light of faith. I will use it in my own ministry.

-Fr. Marcin Szymański, OP

Associate Director – Prince of Peace Newman Center –

University of Washington

ACKNOWLEDGMENTS

TRUE HEART began with a project at Seattle's O'Dea High School in 2014. Mr. Tom Schutte, then director of Campus Ministry, asked me to visit with some of his student leadership team over the course of the year. I was to present ideas on discernment in light of Ignatian Spirituality. I wish to thank Tom and his great students for helping us shape a version of St. Ignatius' life story for this edition. Working with Tom and his students gave us the idea for TRUE HEART. We realized, in light of our meetings, that there are not many good spiritual formation resources for young adults.

The first idea to create something for young adults was to take the adult *Forty Weeks* program and redraft it for young adults. To that end, we worked with over one hundred Jesuit faculty from both Jesuit and Catholic highs across Latin America and the US to gain insights on how they would translate the experience of doing the *Forty Weeks* into ideas for a program for young adults. That Latin American part of this project was facilitated by a former SSI board member, Fr. Hermann Rodriguez, S.J. Thank you, Fr. Hermann.

After the project with Jesuit high school faculty, and when we had a working text, I asked Michael Gurian, founder of the Gurian Institute and New York Times bestseller, to work with me on the initial book concept. He worked with me on language in the exercises that would be appropriate for young adults. He also gave insights on how to pose reflection questions based on the content of the various exercises.

Once we had a working draft of the program incorporating Gurian's suggestions, we launched a beta test of these re-drafted materials in multiple high schools in the US and Latin America, several young adult ministry programs and with seminary students. I wish to thank in particular Andrew Hoelperl and Marcella Nesbitt at McQuaid Jesuit in Rochester for their help with a great group of students. Also, thanks go to Fr. Dan Barnett, rector of Bishop White Seminary in Spokane, Washington and Fr. Derek Lappe, pastor of Mary, Star of the Sea in Bremerton Washington. Also, sincere thanks to Mr. Jose Oyanguren, headmaster of St. Augustine School in Managua, Nicaragua, for his assistance on the beta text with his students and faculty.

Finally, finishing work and refining suggestions came from Matthew Davidson, Ph.D., president for the Institute for Excellence & Ethics in Malinus, NY. My thanks to Matt for his "excellent" suggestions on the final shape of the two books in the series.

DEDICATION

TRUE HEART is dedicated to every young adult who longs for meaning, authenticity, holiness, is committed to timeless truths, and who longs for faithful love in a life that will produce fruit that endures to eternity.

You are the salt of the earth.
But if salt loses its taste,
with what can it be seasoned?
It is no longer good for anything but to be
thrown out and trampled underfoot.
You are the light of the world.
A city set on a mountain cannot be hidden.
Nor do they light a lamp and then put it
under a bushel basket; it is set on a lampstand,
where it gives light to all in the house.
Just so, your light must shine before others,
that they may see your good deeds
and glorify your heavenly Father.

Mt. 5: 13-16

CONTENTS

PREFACE

Dear Friend:

I was eighteen and it was March of my senior year in high-school. Sitting in the basement of our family home I was smoking a cigarette up the fireplace chimney (did not want to let my folks know I was smoking), and watching late-night television. Suddenly, an ad for the Peace Corps came on TV. The commercial showed volunteers working with youth in Africa. I was riveted and said: "That is what I want to do with my life." I never got to sleep that night.

My thoughts moved from a year of service to a life of service—to being a missionary. I was overcome with feelings of love and hope that I had never before experienced. I knew in some way that God was involved with what was happening, but I was also keenly aware that I did not really know God. But I told myself: "God is doing this."

I entered the Jesuit novitiate the following August. The year was 1973. We could only bring one small trunk of personal belongings. One of the items in my trunk was a picture of a bird flying out of a cage. It was how I felt. I had wings for the first time in my life. I was in love and a God I did not yet know had set a fire in my heart. I was on a mission.

Christ did reveal himself to me more clearly during my Ignatian Thirty Day Retreat. I remember that retreat well for its twenty-eight days of rain out of thirty. But it was the contrast of those dark, rainy days in Oregon's Willamette Valley with the brightness and warmth of Christ's love I felt in prayer that stood out the most. After the retreat, Jesus' love for me gained traction and practical expression in the Society of Jesus' devotion to the Sacred Heart of Christ.

But my time in the novitiate was not without crises. Around Easter of my first year, I was convinced I had made a mistake in entering. I told my novice director that I wanted to leave. Being wise, he suggested instead of leaving, that I go home for two weeks and think about it…no hard decisions. I only learned later that one should never make a decision in a time of spiritual desolation, and I was clearly in one at the time.

After two weeks back home, and pondering all the different careers and vocations I might engage, nothing matched the hope, peace and desire I felt in contemplating continuing my life as a Jesuit. So, I took a bus back to the novitiate and resumed my training.

Yet, struggles continued. I was not yet reconciled with the holiness of life I felt called to live, and the reality of my life that felt anything but holy. I did not feel worthy to be a religious. I faced a difficult crossroads. How could I reconcile the intense desire for Christ and giving myself to a religious vocation in light my sinfulness and weakness? God found a way to break the logjam.

I had a powerful dream one night in my second year of novitiate. I was standing, naked, in the palm of a great hand out in the depths of space. Galaxies and stars were all about me. I *knew* that it was in the hand of God that I stood—*naked, known and loved*. God loved me in spite of my failings.

It was the most powerful dream of my life and one of the most *real* experiences I had ever experienced. I woke from the dream knowing it had come from the same source who had given me the desires that night I was watching TV. But now I knew more about this God. Most importantly, I knew that God knew me. I heard the words of Jeremiah 1:5: "Before I formed you in the womb, I knew you."

Almost two years to the date after entering the Society, I pronounced my first vows as a Jesuit. I wanted to commit myself that special day to the path of love that I had experienced. It needed to be a public witness. Yes, I was professing my vows, and that was a public witness. But I felt compelled to do something more.

Each "vow man" was offered a time at the dinner to say something. Many Jesuits and family members attended these events. I decided I wanted to say something about the devotion to the Heart of Christ.

I felt some anxiety contemplating professing my conviction about the importance of the devotion. It wasn't really in style any longer or seen as a needed spiritual practice. I thought I would look foolish and possibly be made fun of. Yet, I felt compelled to say what I believed.

My time to speak came and with apprehension in my heart, I said something to the effect: "I believe it is important for the Society of Jesus that we re-dedicate ourselves to the devotion to the Heart of Christ. If we do this, I think we will be very successful in all our efforts."

I still have Jesuit friends who remind me of my statement that day. So my "witness" did make a lasting impression, and yes, I was kidded, and still am. But the call to have a devotion to the Heart of Christ was affirmed by the Jesuit General, Pedro Arrupe.

Six years after I took vows, and in the final address Arrupe would give before a debilitating stroke silenced him, he confirmed my own convictions.[1]

Jesus is calling you, my friend. He has been since before you were born. He has a plan to make your life take flight—to give you holy wings. He has a mission, rooted in his love, that only you can accomplish. The mission is for your joy. Your "yes" to His loving call can and will transform history.

We created TRUE HEART to give you a path to find your mission. You will need a childlike heart to hear the call, but it will be unmistakable when it comes. Most likely, the call will make you look foolish in the eyes of the world, and even with your friends. But your call is to transform the world with Christ, not conform to its ways.

MAKE AN ACT OF FAITH TO START YOUR JOURNEY

Are you willing to take a leap of faith at the beginning of your TRUE HEART journey? I just mentioned Fr. Pedro Arrupe, S.J, who was superior general of the Jesuits when I entered in 1973. His cause for canonization began in early 2019, nearly twenty-five years after his death. He was indeed a True Heart. He founded the Jesuit Refugee Services and he, more than anyone one, is credited for putting the Jesuits on the path to making Gospel justice part of all our works.

I believe his powerful witness of selflessness was because he had such a strong devotion to the Heart of Christ and Christ's presence in the Blessed Sacrament. He, like Mother Theresa of Calcutta, are known as true servants of justice for the

---

[1] "The Society needs the "dynamis" contained in this symbol and in the reality that it proclaims: the love of the Heart of Christ. Perhaps what we need is an act of ecclesial humility, to accept what the Supreme Pontiffs, the General Congregations and the Generals of the Society have incessantly repeated. And yet, I am convinced that there could be few proofs of the spiritual renewal of the Society so clear as a widespread and vigorous devotion to the Heart of Jesus. Our apostolate would receive new strength and we would see its effects very soon, both in our personal lives and in our apostolic activities." Pedro Arrupe, *Texts on the Heart of Christ* (St. Louis: Institute of Jesuit Sources, 1984). 151.

poor and both were so adamant in a child-like faith in Christ in the presence of the Blessed Sacrament.

After the death of his father in 1926, he soon afterward traveled with his sisters to Lourdes (France), where he witnessed more than one miraculous healing. He took part, as a medical student, in the verification process of one such healing. He witnessed a miraculous healing of a young man "twisted and contorted by Polio." As the bishop passed with the Blessed Sacrament in the monstrance, he blessed the young man who then "rose from the cart cured."

Pedro said that the very same Jesus Christ who had cured so many people in the Gospels cured that young man. The Christ of history and the living Christ in the Blessed Sacrament are one and the same. It was this miracle by the power of Christ in the Blessed Sacrament that promoted Pedro to abandon his medical career and enter the Jesuits three months later, to serve the true Divine Physician. He would later say, "I felt God so close in his miracles that he dragged me after him."

Please pray for a similar healing miracle to take place by the presence of Christ in the Blessed Sacrament to confirm Fr. Arrupe's cause for sainthood.[2] Pray the prayer on the following page for this cause. If you are capable of making this act of faith in a church in the presence of the Blessed Sacrament, do it! It is a perfect way for you to begin your True Heart journey. You are making an act of faith in

---

[2] If you have reason to believe your prayer for healing was answered for a specific person, please communicate any favor received though the intercession of the Servant of God Pedro Arrupe: Postulazione Generale della Compagnia di Gesu/Borgo Santo Spiritu, 4/1-00193, ROME (Italy). Or at: postulazione@sjcuria.org. Remember, the following conditions must be met in the case of physical healings (the most common miracles in canonization cases): The healing must be completely and professionally documented (that is, physician's reports from both before and after the healing); the healing must be attributable solely to one saint's intercession (that is, if you're also praying to Sts. Francis of Assisi, Padre Pio, Francis Xavier and others, it is not going to "count"); the healing must be instantaneous; and the healing has to be permanent (that is, the physical condition cannot relapse). Please also communicate any other favors you believe you have received through the intercession of Servant of God, Fr. Pedro Arrupe, SJ.

Jesus to confirm a True Heart and believing that with Christ, "all things are possible."

Prayer for Pedro Arrupe's Canonization[3]

Dear Lord Jesus,
I believe you are truly present
to me here in the Blessed Sacrament.
Here you are the same person who was present to your disciples
and the people you cured in the Gospel stories.
Here you are the same person in the Blessed Sacrament
who miraculously healed the young man
Pedro Arrupe witnessed at Lourdes.
Through the intercession of Fr. Pedro Arrupe,
Please cause a miraculous cure
through your Blessed Sacrament of
(say the name of the person you want healed
and be specific for the physical healing that is needed).
May this miraculous cure lead to the sainthood
of Fr. Pedro Arrupe and reveal to the world,
like Fr. Arrupe discovered, that you
are truly the living Divine Physician.
I believe that you can affect this healing for
(say the name again and the specific thing needing healing)
and affirm again your healing power and
its promise of eternal life fully present in the Blessed Sacrament.
Thank you for hearing my prayers and answering them
If it serves for Your own glory and praise.

---

3 With Ecclesiastical Approval

May it lead to the conversion of many souls
In honor of the holy and selfless life of Fr. Pedro Arrupe.
Through Christ, our Lord.
AMEN!

Expect miracles of grace, insight and personal transformation all throughout True Heart. Ask Jesus for them. His joy is to make you a True Heart. Pray that Christ "drag you after Him," too!

Peace my friend,

Fr. Bill Watson, S.J.
21 April 2019 Easter Sunday

FOREWORD

A. M. D. G.

"Sacred Heart of Jesus, help me to learn perfect selflessness since this is the only path to you." These are the opening words of the *Prayer of Offering to the Heart of Jesus* written by Saint Claude La Colombière, the Jesuit confessor of Saint Margaret Mary to whom Our Lord revealed the mysteries of His Sacred Heart. In *True Heart: A Way to Selflessness*, Father William Watson, SJ, effectively makes these words his own as he charts a spiritual path from silence through self-knowledge to selflessness.

Silence prepares the way, for otherwise, the ever-increasing distractions of our age would impede our path. Noise and visual images surround us. Screen-viewing consumes much of our waking hours. Sensory overload consequently overwhelms us. Our smartphones, moreover, have outsmarted us, making us dumb. What we once retained in our memory we have now transferred to our phones and allowed them to think for us.

Keeping us wired 24/7, our cell phones have also made us more anxious and depressed. By significantly raising our stress levels, this digital cacophony is undermining our physical, mental and spiritual health. Today, the 1984 movie *The Terminator* seems oddly prophetic. For machines, that we have built, are, if you will, killing us. As a young adult today you are particularly susceptible to the adverse effects of modern technology, for you have never known a world without the Internet.

In particular, social media ironically tends to make us less social and, hence, more self-centered. Such technology-driven self-centeredness is ultimately a dead end. The way out is the way to selflessness. Father Watson's contemporary spiritual exercises in the Ignatian tradition map out for young adults a path from life-sapping self-centeredness, and the loneliness it creates, into a life-giving selflessness and connectedness to others and to the Lord.

The Christian tradition has always prized silence where the soul communes with its Creator. But today, more and more, neuroscientists, medical professionals, Silicon Valley technicians and non-religious organizations have also begun to acknowledge the benefits to be gained from meditation and "mindfulness."

They encourage us to find technology-free spaces for the sake of our well-being. Father Watson himself invites young adults to find a quiet, technology-free place apart from this world's constant distractions in order to gain self-knowledge in Our Lord's company.

He counsels you to unhook "from technology so that you can hear your heart" (from the *Introduction*). This unhooking entails being still and knowing the God who has created us in His own Image. Jesus Himself, the visible Image of the invisible Father, shows us the way to authentic self-knowledge.

On this account, Father Watson invites you to speak prayerfully with Jesus and indeed to imitate Jesus' own nocturnal prayer by keeping vigil during the quiet hours of the night when, in the silent sanctuary of your heart, spiritual discourse becomes most intimate.

A true heart pulsates with pure love. But sadly, if we are honest with ourselves, we will have to admit that our loves are not always pure. They are, in fact, quite often self-seeking. Even the saints lamented the times when they had fallen short in their ardent desire to love God with an undivided heart. That is why Saint Claude La Colombière himself prays: "Teach me what I must do to attain the purity of your love, the desire for which you have inspired in me. I feel powerless ever to succeed in this aim without a very exceptional light and special help that I can only expect from you." Jesus alone gives us the grace of pure love. In giving us that grace, He also calls us to cooperate with it.

Cooperating with His grace, we enter deeply into His love for us, the source of all pure love. The experience of His selfless, crucified love unmasks our self-centeredness and moves our wounded hearts to contrition. Sorrow for our sins is the necessary first step toward true repentance and conversion. Such frank self-knowledge also entails an honest admission of our own inability— or, in Saint Claude's words, our powerlessness—to break free, alone and unaided, from all that binds us interiorly.

Here again, we pray with Saint Claude: "Accomplish your will in me, Lord. I know that I resist it, but it seems to me that I would truly like not to resist. It is you who will have to do it all, divine Heart of Jesus Christ." Yes, Christ's grace alone paves the pathway to freedom.

This journey to selflessness, this journey to discover our true heart in the True Heart of Jesus, leads us "to rest and find a new way to live our life" (from the *Introduction*). Whereas self-centeredness is always a matter of our turning away from God, the journey, to which Father Watson invites his readers, entails an ever more complete turning toward God. Only in that "turning toward," which begins in grace, does Jesus' light dispel our darkness and the peace, that He alone can give, abide within us.

This world's peace" only anesthetizes us and nothing more. The blue light shining from the screens, that we hold in our hands or before which we sit, saps our energy rather than restores our strength. It hypnotizes rather than illuminates.

By diverting its gaze from these seductive rays, the true heart finds peace when it beholds Christ and bathes in His light. The true heart gladly acknowledges before Jesus in the words of Saint Claude La Colombière that "the glory of my sanctification will be yours alone, and it is for that reason alone that I wish to desire perfection." What is this desired perfection? It is to rest in God. As Saint Augustine of Hippo eloquently observes in his *Confessions,* because God has created us for Himself, our hearts remain restless until they rest in Him. Truly, in the end, only the selfless heart experiences enduring peace.

True Heart: A Way to Selflessness is a journey worth taking. For those of you who undertake it wholeheartedly, it will turn out to be a marvelous, spiritually life-giving adventure.

These spiritual exercises are indeed a treasure map to a treasure buried in the field of your innermost self. That treasure, placed there by God in whose Image we have been created, is the gift of Christ's peace experienced both in time and for all eternity.

Father Joseph Carola, S.J.
Gregorian University, Rome, 21 January 2019
Memorial of Saint Agnes, Roman Virgin and Martyr

INTRODUCTION

THE TRUE HEART JOURNEY TO SELFLESSNESS

St Ignatius Loyola awoke to his true heart at the age of thirty. He was given the grace to see how two different sets of fantasies, portraying two possible directions his life could take, were fundamentally different from each other. The first set of fantasies he described as "vain" and were focused on his ego and achieving fame (self-centered). The second set of fantasies he described as "holy" and focused on serving Christ and doing good works (selfless).

Both the self-centered and selfless fantasies entertained him while he actively fantasized their possibilities. But one day he was given grace to notice a difference. When he set the self-centered fantasies aside, he felt dry and dissatisfied. When he set the selfless fantasies aside, he felt peaceful and content. He was given to understand that the selfless fantasies that left him peaceful and content were his "true heart," and from that day forward he pursued those dreams and fantasies.

There are a million stories in each life but each life only has two possible directions: towards God and the light (selflessness) or away from God and the light (self-centeredness). The goal of True Heart is to help you, in the short space of ten weeks, understand the two fundamentally different directions your life might take. Only one direction can make you feel content and peaceful. Only one direction is your True Heart.

To understand your True Heart, and the great mission you have been chosen for in this life, each day of the ten weeks will have set spiritual exercises. Nearly half the allotted time for spiritual exercises is simply unhooking from technology so you can hear your heart!

Thank you for taking this journey to your True Heart, and I invite you to:

Do your daily training to invite Christ,
the Divine Physician, into your heart.

Pray for everyone seeking to live life as a *TRUE HEART*.

Thank God that you have been invited to participate with
Christ in His Great Work of Reconciliation

Commit to daily training in order to realize your
goal of being a person who is joyful, peaceful and anchored in your true
identity—your True Heart

Be a Leader who helps others find their way
to the only person in the Cosmos who is
The Way, The Truth and The Life—Christ the original TRUE HEART.
Train daily in all your thoughts, words and deeds.
And Do Not Be Afraid!

ℰ

*There are very few who realize what God would make of them
if they abandoned themselves entirely to His hands, and let
themselves be formed by His grace. A thick and shapeless tree
trunk would never believe that it could become a statue,
admired as a miracle of sculpture...and would never consent to
submit itself to the chisel of the sculptor who, as St. Augustine
says, sees by his genius what he can make of it. Many people
who, we see, now scarcely live as Christians, do not understand
that they could become saints, if they would let themselves be
formed by the grace of God, if they did not ruin His plans by
resisting the work which He wants to do.*[4]

St. Ignatius Loyola

---

[4] Paul Doncoeur, SJ, *The Heart of Ignatius*, (Baltimore: Helicon, 1959), 34.

TRUE HEART
Spiritual Exercises

Daily exercises will help you to build your faith, knowledge of your vocation and discernment ability—your ability to discover your true heart. Thus you can become more peaceful and content. The rituals of True Heart comprise the highly effective methods St. Ignatius developed many centuries ago to discover his own True Heart. The program consists daily of:

THREE PERIODS
THREE PRAYERS
THREE EXERCISES

Each day True Heart invites you to take three special periods of quiet, tech-free "spiritual time," engage three different prayer disciplines and do three spiritual exercises. They are described here:

THREE PERIODS

When I Awake in the Morning—20 Minutes Total

For the first twenty minutes after getting up in the morning, keep free of all media and technology so that your heart has the necessary quiet to access the spiritual world. Make your bed, shower and get ready for the day but be quiet and reflective, thinking about the day ahead.

When I Go to Bed at Night—20 Minutes Total

Turn off all technology and media twenty minutes before going to bed. This will help you access the spiritual world and also sleep better. Use this time also to spend 1-2 minutes to do your Training Journal.

Day True Heart Time—45 Minutes Total

Have forty-five minutes in the day where you use no media or technology. The time should be contiguous and not several non-sequential time segments added together. You can do your fifteen-minute True Heart prayer, read the reflection exercise for the day, walk, exercise or rest but be alone, quiet and reflective.

THREE PRAYERS

TRUE HEART Prayer—15 Minutes Total

Take fifteen minutes to do the True Heart spiritual discipline reflecting on Creation, Presence, Memory, Mercy and Eternity. Do it mid-day, mid-afternoon or just after the evening meal or during your Day True Heart Time. Use one of the MP3 meditations found in the MEMBER section of sacredstory.net website under True Heart Resources. Membership is free.

Find a quiet place apart, a place where you will not be disturbed by family, friends, of the things of the world. Bring with you any specific annoyances or strong emotional events you experienced today. Bring also your self-centered and selfless daydreams.

When I Awake in the Morning for 1-2 Minutes Total

When your alarm goes off, keep your eyes closed and "feel" the day before you. Are you anxious or hopeful? Ask Christ to help you overcome the specific anxieties you experience. Thank Him for the hopes you identify and the graces you will be given that day. Before opening your eyes, offer your day to God and by praying for protection to St. Michael, Christ's Lead Guardian in the battle against evil. [5]

When I Go to Bed at Night for 1-2 Minutes Total

Before falling asleep, pray for your True Heart companion and mentor by name. Feel your heart to determine if you are you anxious or hopeful. Ask Christ to help you overcome your specific anxieties. Thank Christ for the hopes you

---

[5] Invite God to be with you all day long:

Traditional Morning Offering
O Jesus, through the Immaculate Heart of Mary,
I offer you my prayers, works, joys, and sufferings of this day
for all the intentions of your Sacred Heart,
in union with the Holy Sacrifice of the Mass throughout the world,
for the salvation of souls, the reparation of sins, the reunion of all Christians,
and in particular for the intentions of the Holy Father this month.
Amen.

I Arise Today
I arise to-day:
might of Heaven
brightness of Sun, whiteness of Snow
splendour of Fire, speed of Light, swiftness of Wind,
depth of Sea stability of Earth, firmness of Rock.
I arise to-day :
Might of God, Power of God
Wisdom of God, Eye of God
Ear of God, Word of God
Hand of God, Path of God
Shield of God, Host of God
(From *The Book of Cerne*, 9th C)

St Michael Prayer Before Opening Eyes
Holy Michael, the Archangel, defend us in battle.
Be our safeguard against the wickedness and snares of the devil.
May God rebuke him, we humbly pray; and do you,
O Prince of the heavenly host, by the power of God cast into hell Satan and all the evil spirits
who wander through the world seeking the ruin of souls.
Amen.

identify. Ask God to be present in your dreams. End by asking Christ to stand watch through the night.

THREE EXERCISES

Spiritual Exercise—15-20 Minutes

Each day True Heart gives you a specific spiritual exercise. You can do this exercise in the morning, evening or during the day quiet times.

Reflection Exercise—1-3 Minutes

Most of True Heart's spiritual exercises have reflection questions. Use your Log to jot these reflections down. You can do this at the end of your spiritual exercise or at the end of the day during your quiet time.

Journal Exercise—1-2 Minutes

Once you begin the True Heart training you will be aware of new spiritual movements in your life. Briefly writing two items your True Heart Exercise Journal will help you build the discipline to understand your spiritual life and begin to discern the difference between vain and holy fantasies.

On the "holy" end of the scale, you are looking for gratitude, hope, and peace linked to your True Heart and the daydreams and fantasies coming from the Divine-Inspirer—(selfless dreams). So look for those fantasies, dreams and actions that increase your faith, your hope and your love of God and your neighbor.

On the "vain" end of the scale, you are looking for patterns of sin, compulsion and addiction linked to your false heart and the daydreams and fantasies coming from the counter-inspirer (self-centered dreams). So look for those fantasies, dreams and actions that decrease your faith, hope and love of God and neighbor. Be brief in your two items but specific, and address Jesus in your notes. Only you will see this journal so strive for honesty. Here is an example to help you focus:

Vain & Self-Centered:

Jesus, my desire to be number one made me envious
and dismissive of others.

Holy and Selfless:

Jesus, the argument I witnessed today made me realize I want to help people
find peaceful ways to resolve problems.

Journal Weekly Summary

At week's end, read over your short daily journal entries and decide which vain and which holy fantasy/daydream/action was the one you considered the most significant for the week and write them down in your journal.

Journal Monthly Summary

At month's end, read over your short weekly journal summaries and decide which vain and which holy fantasy/daydream/action was the one you considered the most significant for the month and write them down in your journal.

ADDITIONAL ELEMENTS
True Heart Companion and/or Mentor—10 Minutes Total
(1 or 2 times a week)

If I am doing True Heart with others I know, I will consider touching base with my True Heart Companion once or twice a week. I will ask how they are doing and if anyone needs help or prayers. They will do the same for me. We will help and pray for each other.

True Heart Mentor—20 Minutes Total Per-Month

I will consult an older mentor if I have any difficulties I can't resolve on my own. True Heart Mentor—20 Minutes Total (1 time per month).

NIGHT VIGILS

The Night Vigil meditations are modeled on Ignatian Spiritual Exercises. You use your senses (imagination, smell, sight etc.) to enter the Gospel stories and "see" them in your mind's eye. They provide a step by step way to enter the Gospel stories. However, feel free in praying them differently if you find them too scripted for your prayer style. We recommend doing them at night to model some of St. Ignatius' most important moments in his conversion process. People find them very powerful ways to integrate the daily prayer experiences and draw close to Christ. We know you will benefit from them profoundly and these will prepare you for the Night Vigil that concludes the TRUE HEART journey.

TRUE HEART EXERCISE LOG

To help you keep track of your spiritual development, fill out this training report daily. It will help you to see the trainings you complete and don't complete. You can find a free PDF booklet version of these daily reports for the whole program at https://sacredstory.net/true-heart-young-adult-program/.

THREE PERIODS

1. Morning True Heart Time—20 Minutes Total

Location_____ I Trained Yes___ No___ (If no, why?_____)

2. Evening True Heart Time—20 Minutes Total

Location_____ I Trained Yes___ No___ (If no, why?_____)

3. Day True Heart Time—A Contiguous 45 Minutes

Location_____ I Trained Yes___ No___ (If no, why?_____)

THREE PRAYERS

1. When I Awake in the Morning Prayer—2 Minutes Total

Location_____ I Trained Yes___ No___ (If no, why?_____)

2. TRUE HEART Prayer—Fifteen Minutes Total

Location_____ I Trained Yes___ No___ (If no, why?_____)

3. As I Lay Down to Sleep Prayer—2 Minutes Total

Location_____ I Trained Yes___ No___ (If no, why?_____)

THREE EXERCISES

1. Daily Spiritual Exercise—15-20 Minutes Daily

Location_____ I Trained Yes___ No___ (If no, why?_____)

2. Daily Spiritual Reflection Exercise—1-3 Minutes Daily

Location_____ I Trained Yes___ No___ (If no, why?_____)

3. Exercise Journal—1-2 Minutes Daily

Location_____ I Trained Yes___ No___ (If no, why?_____)

JOURNAL ENTRIES

-- A "vain, self-centered" fantasy or action that decreased my faith, hope and love of God and neighbor.

---A "holy, self-less" fantasy or action that increased my faith, hope and love of God and neighbor.

ROADBLOCKS?

If you reach a point True Heart training where you think you can't continue, here is my advice. Jump to the last chapter, The Rest of Your Life and read Abide in Me. I placed this chapter at the end to encourage people to commit to a life-long process of True Heart discernment and prayer. But sometimes, that encouragement is necessary to simply complete the process that will carry you for life. Just keep trying and remember: Do Not Be Afraid!

Your heart is prepared and you are ready to begin True Heart training. Trust your heart! Part of trusting your heart is focusing on each day's disciplines and not worrying about the future ones.

So Remember: Do not train ahead, don't look ahead. Stay in the present moment. Take each day, and each training as it comes. Say to yourself, "I can't do True Heart training better by going faster."

Now, before beginning your journey, say these statements aloud, slowly.

I am starting a Relationship that will
carry me for the rest of my life.

I will be faithful to my training and
open my heart to God every day.

I trust that God will lead me to selflessness
in knowing my True Heart.

I thank Jesus for giving me the companions and mentors I will need in the
journey of life.

I believe that Jesus always awaits me with His
Strength, Grace, Mercy and Love
even when I am self-centered.

What do I need for this journey?

A generous true heart.
The willingness to train daily.
The humility to always ask God for help.

໑

WEEK 1

DAY ONE

Spiritual Exercise for Day True Heart Time

Take a moment to ask God for this grace: "Lord, open me to the knowledge of my own heart."

The heart is where the important work of prayer takes place. The mind reveals facts but the heart reveals the truth, your innermost being. The "heart" is the word used in Scripture for the most important aspects of the human condition.

Listen to the passages below and "listen" to which statements strike your own heart. Discover which ones have the strongest impact, stir you, give you hope. Notice the ones that feel like they are "just for you."

Mark those and write in your journal the reason you think they are meaningful for you.

Here are the examples:

✠   The heart reveals the state of corruption caused by sin [6]

---

[6] (Gen 6:5; Jer 17:9-10; Mt 15:9). There is no need to read the Scripture passages during your 15-minute prayer periods. If your heart leads you to read these Scripture passages apart from the 15-minute prayer periods, you are encouraged to follow your heart!

✠ The heart is where the process of conversion and forgiveness takes place. [7]

✠ A True Heart enables one to see God.[8]

✠ The heart is the center of compassion.[9]

✠ The heart is the vessel holding the secrets that illuminate the true meaning of life (Mt 6:21; Lk 24:32; Ps 85:9).

✠ The heart is defined as the center of human consciousness... [10]

✠ The heart perceives love as the ultimate end, gift, and purpose of being (1 Cor 13).

✠ The testimony of Christ in Scripture speaks to the heart's desire for innocence., .[11]

✠ Christ gives the conviction that He can be found in hearts who seek Him [12]

Seek *knowledge of the heart* and ask God for the grace to open a pathway to your heart. Seek, also, knowledge of God's heart, present in Christ's Sacred Heart. This grace will help to unite your heart to the heart of Christ.

Say out loud: "Lord, open me to the knowledge of my heart."

Every day, pay close attention to what your heart senses and believes.

---

[7] (Ez 36:26; Mt 18:35; Rom 2:29)

[8] (Mt 5:8)

[9] (Lk 7:13)

[10] (Heb 4:12-13)

[11] (Mt 11:28-30.)

[12] (Lk 11:9-11).

DAY TWO

Spiritual Exercise for Day True Heart Time
True Heart Affirmations

Be Not Afraid:

Fear comes from the enemy of my human nature.

This is an example of the kind of affirmations you will use in various parts of your True Heart journey. As your first spiritual disciplines of this training, take this day to speak aloud and listen to these *Affirmations.*

As you do this, be attentive to all the persons, events and issues in your life. Be especially attentive to the affirmations that might stimulate fear or anxiety and those that stimulate hope or gratitude. Notice *how* and *if* the affirmation connects to an issue that is causing those feelings.

As you do this, be attentive to all the persons, events and issues in your life. Be especially attentive to the affirmations that might stimulate fear or anxiety. Notice *how* and *if* the affirmation connects to an issue that is causing those feelings.

Like all good training, you want to focus on the things that build up your courage and strength or undermine it. Focusing on things that stimulate fear or anxiety will help you uncover the most important human and spiritual elements holding you back.

So listen to the affirmations and feel what you feel. Experience deeper, lasting peace as you let difficulties arise and allow the Divine Physician to heal you.

Remember: We have nothing to fear with Christ by our side. Take as long as you desire to reflect on True Heart *Affirmations*. We give two days for this spiritual exercise.

TRUE HEART *Affirmations—Awakening—Say Them Aloud*

My selfless path to *TRUE HEART* takes a lifetime.

Be Not Afraid:

Fear comes from the enemy of my human nature.

The pathway to God's peace and healing

runs through my heart's

brokenness, sin, fear, anger and grief.

God resolves all my problems with time and patience.

ඥ

There are just two ways to cope with the

difficulties I discover in my life.

One leads to selflessness, one to self-centeredness.

I will choose selflessness.

ඥ

Nothing is ever impossible for God!

TRUE HEART selflessness leads to my

freedom and authenticity, but does not always make me feel happy.

ඥ

My life's greatest tragedies can be transformed

into my life's major blessings.

27

Times of peace and hope always give way
to times of difficulty and stress.
Times of difficulty and stress always give way
to times of peace and hope.

☙

I will not tire of asking God for help since
God delights in my asking.
The urge to stop *TRUE HEART* training always
comes before my greatest breakthroughs.

☙

God gives me insights, not because I am better
than others, but because I am loved.

The insights and graces I need to move forward in
life's journey unfold at the right time.

☙

My personal engagement with *TRUE HEART* accomplishes, through Christ, a
work of eternal significance.
Inspirations can have a divine or a demonic source.
I pray for the grace to remember how
to discern one from the other.

☙

Christ, who has walked before me, shares my every burden.
Christ, who has walked before me,
will help me resolve every crisis.
Christ, who has walked before me, knows my every hope.
Christ, who has walked before me, knows everything I suffer.
Christ, who walks before me, will always
lead me home to safety.

DAY THREE

Spiritual Exercise for Day True Heart Time
True Heart Affirmations

Remember: We have nothing to fear with Christ by our side. Take as long as you desire to reflect on True Heart *Affirmations*. We give two days for this spiritual exercise.

TRUE HEART Affirmations—Awakening—Say Them Aloud

I will strive to curb temptations to react to people and events.
I will ask myself what causes my self-centeredness,
anger and irritation at people and events.

I will seek to identify the source of my
self-centeredness, anger and irritation.

I will give thanks for what makes me self-centered,
angry and upset for identifying the sources
will help to set me free.

I will strive to listen, watch and pray;
listen, watch and pray.

I will listen, watch and pray!

∽

Everyone has been mortally wounded
spiritually, psychologically, and physically by Original Sin and the loss of
selflessness in paradise.

Journeying with Christ to the roots of my sins and addictions to technology,
videogames, shopping, pornography, exercise, alcohol, or other substances
will help break their grip.

I will not waste time worrying about my sins
and failures but rather, I will use my time wisely and ask God to help me to
understand the source of my sins and failings.

I will trust that Christ came to heal
all my self-centered wounds.

∽

I alone control Christ's ability to transform
my life into a selfless *TRUE HEART*.
The process begins when I ask for the grace and honestly name my sins and
addictions.
The process continues when I invite Christ
to illuminate my selfishness.
Only God's grace and mercy can
give me a selfless *TRUE HEART*.

DAY FOUR

Spiritual Exercise for Day True Heart Time
St. Ignatius' Story Part One: A Life Upended

A Self-Centered Person

Until his thirtieth year, Ignatius Loyola was unconscious of the sacredness of his life. Instead, he was sincerely devoted to life's pleasures and vanities. He was a gambling addict, sexually self-indulgent, arrogant, hotheaded and insecure. In short, he was very self-centered and narcissistic.

By our contemporary measures, Ignatius' family was dysfunctional. Was Ignatius a possible candidate for sainthood? It did not look promising. But God does not judge by human standards. It is in God's mercy to pursue all who have fallen asleep through sin, addiction and selfishness. God judges the heart. With unbounded grace and patient mercy, God reaches into the ruins that sin makes of our lives and transforms them into *Sacred Stories.*

Ignatius, with all his narcissism, psychological problems and sinful vices, was awakened by God's great love. A failed military campaign that left him with a shattered leg forced him into a lengthy convalescence back at Loyola castle, his family home. Ignatius' time of recuperation provided an opportunity for Christ to shine a light on much more serious and life-threatening wounds that were spiritual, emotional and psychological in nature.

These more serious wounds were gradually evolved from a destructive, sinful narcissism. Contributing to his problems were the facts that Ignatius' mother died when he was an infant and his father died when he was sixteen and his family had a history of infidelity and violent behavior. Even his brother who was a Catholic priest had five children. Human families and the family of the Church have always had problems.

For thirty years Ignatius' narcissism had rendered him unconscious to his true human nature and oblivious to his life as *a TRUE HEART*. The pleasures he indulged in and the power he wielded functioned like a narcotic to numb the pain of his hidden spiritual and psychological wounds. His sinful vices and self-indulgent pleasures blinded him to his authentic human nature. Yet God saw his life could be fruitful if Ignatius awakened to his conscience.

God's grace reached into the sinful and chaotic heart of Ignatius' life and awakened in him a desire for innocence. His long-buried aspirations for living authentically suddenly became his prime motivation. He noticed it first while recovering from his wounds at Loyola. He became aware of new desires and a different energy while he daydreamed in reading stories of Christ and the saints. Pondering the saints' lives he imagined himself living a different, selfless life.

He compared these new daydreams to his former vain, narcissistic daydreams. The old daydreams drew energy from a life of sin, addiction and vice. The new daydreams of selfless generosity produced their own very different energy. Ignatius noticed a significant difference between the two sets of daydreams and the energies they created in his heart. The vain fantasies entertained him when he was thinking about them. But he noticed that when he set them aside, he felt him empty and unsatisfied.

The new holy daydreams also entertained him when he was thinking about them. Yet when he set these aside, he remained content and felt an enduring calm and quiet joy. By paying close attention to the different moods these two energies created in his heart, and discerning their difference, Ignatius discovered and popularized spiritual discernment and created a system of spiritual disciplines that transformed his life and the history of Christian spirituality. Here is his discovery in a graphic chart:

Hearing the Voice of Conscience

Ignatius discovered that the new, selfless aspirations were influenced by Divine inspirations. He further discovered that these inspirations reflected his true human nature. He discovered too that the vain fantasies deadened his conscience. His narcissistic daydreams led him away from enduring peace because they masked his true heart. The old daydreams and fantasies were powerful, ego-affirming, and familiar but ultimately left him empty and unsatisfied.

Ignatius was awakened to the emotional wisdom and spiritual truth of his new daydreams. He became aware of the significant damage that his old lifestyle had done to both himself and others. What had been awakened in him was the divine gift of conscience. With an awakened conscience, Ignatius experienced profound regret and sorrow for having wasted so much of his life on self-indulgent pleasures and fantasies, seductions that could never bring him lasting peace and satisfaction. He began to understand that living in pleasure and fantasy destroyed his True Heart and silenced his deepest desires.

Divine inspiration inspired Ignatius to seek forgiveness for wasting his life and his innocence. Grace enabled Ignatius to take responsibility for his sins against God and his True Heart. Divine inspiration provided Ignatius with the desire, energy, and courage to renounce the thoughts, words, and deeds of his sinful habits. Grace, received through the Sacrament of Reconciliation, heightened Ignatius' consciousness and enabled him to imagine a new path for his life and new ways to express his gifts and talents.

As usually happens when people respond to the grace of conversion, Ignatius' new aspirations confused and disconcerted many of his closest family members and friends. Nonetheless, he acted on these aspirations. Ignatius was now able to understand a path to God, a *pattern of conversion* that countless thousands would imitate.

What would this kind of conversion feel like to you, now, in the third millennium?

Have you felt grace before? When? Describe that feeling and that incident in your journal.

Have you felt something very passionately that confused the people close to you? As you look back on it, was that feeling something you regret now? Was it something you realize has helped form you into who you are?

Explore that incident and that feeling and maybe let it be your journal entry tonight.

In light of St. Ignatius's story, briefly describe one pattern of self-centeredness and one pattern of selflessness that you note in yourself.

DAY FIVE

Spiritual Exercise for Day True Heart Time

St Ignatius' Story Part Two:
A Journey to a Selfless TRUE HEART

Ignatius in Control

Ignatius' decisive and enduring commitment to his conversion launched him directly into the center of his heart's brokenness and the pride masking those wounds. After leaving home Ignatius traveled to Montserrat and spent three days reviewing his life. It was at this time that he made a general confession of all his past sinful deeds. In this written confession Ignatius consciously detailed his sinful attitudes, behaviors and passions: gambling addiction, sexual self-indulgence, arrogance, and violent outbursts of temper. It took all three days to write the story of his past life.

But Ignatius started to confess and re-confess past sins multiple times, never feeling he had gotten to the bottom of his immoral deeds. This excruciating spiritual and psychological torment lasted for months. He was so anguished by his obsessive guilt that numerous times he wanted to commit suicide by throwing himself off the cliff where he prayed.

Finally, exhausted and disgusted with his efforts, he realized he intensely despised the spiritual life he was living. Ignatius had an urgent and compelling desire to "stop it!" Reflecting on the temptation to walk away from his new Christian life, Ignatius received an insight that the burdensome, destructive habit of re-confessing past sins was rooted in a pride to try and save himself. This pride forced him to his knees. On seeing this he "awoke as if from a dream," and was given the grace to stop the habit.

It is here that Ignatius admits his powerlessness to save himself and surrenders control of his life to God—he becomes selfless. This opposite of pride is selflessness.

This harrowing crisis taught Ignatius a most vital lesson about counter-inspirations. The willpower and resolute commitment to live virtuously for the rest of his life could be manipulated and turned against him by means of subtle *inspirations*. What seemed like a holy, pious, and noble practice—a serious approach to confession—evolved into a damaging habit that made him loathe his spiritual life, and in frustration, *inspired* him to abandon it. He learned that the counter-inspirations of the enemy of his human nature could act like "an angel of light." These inspirations appear holy but when followed, they end in disaster, turning one from God and toward a self-centered pride to stay in control your life.

God led Ignatius through this distorted evolution back to the lost innocence of his true human nature—his true heart of selflessness. To get there Ignatius had to confront his pattern of spiritual and psychological distortions signified by his self-centered pride. It was a mighty castle that he had built on the shifting sands of a child's wounded innocence, on a child's lonely, broken heart. God provided Ignatius the inspiration and grace to allow that castle to crumble. The shattering of his powerful defenses and the unmasking of his self-centered, narcissistic pattern proved to be the tipping point of Ignatius' entire conversion process.

Ignatius' conversion from his anti-story of selfishness and his full awakening to his selfless *TRUE HEART* was not a single event but rather a gradual process. His full evolution from a vain egomaniac to a selfless saint took the rest of his life.

A proud, dissolute, insecure, self-centered narcissist finally found peace and contentment in God's full love, acceptance, mercy, and forgiveness. Interestingly enough, this happened in and through Ignatius' sinful, self-centered pride and perhaps even because of them! What marred his early life became the very source of his strength and sanctity—his *TRUE HEART*. Ignatius discovered, like St. Paul, that in his weaknesses and sin, he was strong in Christ (2 Cor 12:10). The same conversion from self-centeredness to selflessness awaits us all.

Recall the two parts of St. Ignatius' *TRUE HEART* narrative.

1) What spontaneously evoked *anxiety* in me about my own self-centeredness as I listened to St. Ignatius' story? I will reflect on why my anxiety was provoked and the particular type of self-centeredness I discovered. In my notebook, I will record what evoked my anxiety and why.

2) What spontaneously evoked *inspiration* and hope in me about my own selflessness as I listened to Ignatius' conversion story? I will reflect on why I was inspired or hopeful and the particular type of selflessness I discovered. In my notebook I will record what inspired me and why.

DAY SIX

Spiritual Exercise for Day True Heart Time

For your True Heart Day Time recall the two parts of St. Ignatius' *TRUE HEART* narrative. Read the three questions below and in the space of one sentence write a response in your log book for today.

1). What spontaneously evoked *anxiety* in me as I listened to Ignatius' story? I will reflect on why my anxiety was provoked. In a single sentence, I will write what evoked my anxiety and why.

2). As I listened to Ignatius' conversion story, what *inspired* or gave me *hope* about my life? I will reflect on why I was inspired or hopeful. In a single sentence I will write in my notebook what inspired me and why.

3). "Like Ignatius, have I discovered the one area of my life that convinces me, beyond any doubt, that I cannot save myself, and must rely on God to save me is_____."

DAY SEVEN

Spiritual Exercise for Day True Heart Time

For your True Heart time, read the following poem attributed to the Jesuit, Fr. Pedro Arrupe. It is about the most important thing in the world: falling in love forever!

FALL IN LOVE

Nothing is more practical than
finding God, than
falling in Love
in a quite absolute, final way.
What you are in love with,
what seizes your imagination, will affect everything.
It will decide
what will get you out of bed in the morning,
what you do with your evenings,
how you spend your weekends,
what you read, whom you know,
what breaks your heart,
and what amazes you with joy and gratitude.
Fall in Love, stay in love,
and it will decide everything.

At the end of your reading, write in your journal what would make you fall in love "in a quite absolute, final way?"

Would it be a type of person, a commitment, a mission or something else?

Write your responses below or in your journal.

What amazed you about your response(s)?

Night Vigil Week 1

ALONE AT NIGHT WITH JESUS

Jesus Goes Up Alone on a Mountain to Pray—James Tissot (1836-1902)

Do only one section at a time. Do not read ahead but stay with each section until you feel inclined to move on.

Spend 15-45 minutes on this meditation

I. Let yourself be mindful of the presence of Christ Jesus in the Blessed Sacrament. Spend a minute or two to get in a position of prayer that allows you to relax but at the same time stay alert. As you repose in this way, ask God to keep you open to your own life and God's love for the whole retreat. As a way of asking for this

41

grace of openness, pray the *Triple Colloquy* below. Stay with this as long as you are able to remain engaged in this prayer. Move ahead as your heart suggests. Rest with Jesus as his disciples might have at the end of a day of ministry and preaching.

II. "Now it was about this time that he (Jesus) went out into the hills to pray: and he spent the whole night in prayer to God." (Lk. 6:12)

Imagine the kind of place Jesus went to so he could be alone. Spend some time to create in your own imagination the location as you envision it. Pay attention to all things: the color of the evening sky and stars, the rocks and vegetation, the trees and the views from the hills, what the evening air felt like. Place yourself in the scene at a distance from Jesus so he cannot detect your presence. Move on when your heart suggests.

III. After a while, imagine Jesus notices you alone in that place. Watch as he approaches you and see him sit quietly next to you. He knows you are beginning a journey and after a while, he asks you why you have decided to come. What do you say to him as asks you this? Spend some time telling him your hopes and fears. You know he understands what you are saying and the depth of your desires and concerns. The two of you just sit quietly in each other's presence. Stay here for as long as you like. Before you leave the place, ask him for the grace to stay open to what he wants for you to receive from the retreat.

IV. As you walk down the hill, go back to your room slowly praying the words of the *Our Father*.

TRIPLE COLLOQUY OF SAINT IGNATIUS

First Colloquy, or conversation, will be with Mary. Speak with Mary, using your own words, asking her to obtain from her Son the grace of selflessness to be open to the Spirit working inside you. When you finish this conversation, pray the *Hail Mary* slowly, thinking of the words and the person to whom you are praying.

> *Hail Mary, full of grace The Lord is with thee.*
> *Blessed art thou amongst women*
> *and blessed is the fruit of thy womb, Jesus.*
> *Holy Mary, Mother of God, Pray for us sinners,*
> *Now and at the hour of our death.*

> *Amen.*

Second Colloquy, or conversation, will be with Jesus. Speak directly to Jesus, asking him to request his Father for the same graces as above. When you finish your conversation, pray the *Anima Christi* slowly, thinking of the words and the person to whom you are praying.

> *Soul of Christ, sanctify me. Body of Christ, save me.*
> *Blood of Christ, fill me. Water from the side of Christ wash me.*
> *Passion of Christ, strengthen me. O Good Jesus, hear me.*
> *Within thy wounds, hide me. Permit me not to be separated from thee.*
> *From the wicked foe, defend me. At the hour of my death, call me,*
> *And bid me come to thee that with thy saints*
> *I may praise thee forever and ever.*

> *Amen.*

Third Colloquy, or conversation, will be with God the Father. Ask the Father directly in your own words to give you the graces as described above. When you finish, pray the *Our Father,* thinking of the words and the person to whom you are praying.

Our Father, Who art in heaven Hallowed be thy name.
Thy Kingdom come. Thy will be done,
On earth as it is in heaven.
Give us this day our daily bread,
And forgive us our trespasses,
As we forgive those who trespass against us.
Lead us not into temptation,
But deliver us from evil.

Amen.

WEEK 2

DAY ONE

Spiritual Exercise for Day True Heart Time
Gospel of Mark Chapter One:

Read the text from Mark One below (or in your Bible). In place of the sentence that says:" Jesus said to them," read it with your name in place of "them." I have provided the original passage and then, just below it, the passage with the names left blank so that you can insert yours and others name.

The Call of the First Disciples

As he passed by the Sea of Galilee, he saw Simon and his brother Andrew casting their nets into the sea; they were fishermen.

Jesus said to them, "Come after me, and I will make you fishers of men." Then they abandoned their nets and followed him.

He walked along a little farther and saw James, the son of Zebedee, and his brother John. They too were in a boat mending their nets. Then he called them. So they left their father Zebedee in the boat along with the hired men and followed him.

Fill in your name and others who come to mind.

As he passed by the Sea of Galilee, he saw _____ casting a net into the sea.

Jesus said to _____, "Come after me, and I will make you fishers of men."

Then _____ abandoned the net and followed him.

He walked along a little farther and saw _____, the son/daughter of _____ who was in a boat mending nets. Then he called _____ so _____ left the other workers and followed him.

Hear Jesus' call. In your imagination, do you follow Jesus?

The others had to leave some people behind. In your imagination do you have to leave anyone behind to follow the call to be with Jesus?

As always with True Heart, feel free to write notes in your journal, or speak aloud your thoughts, if seeing the words on paper, or hearing them spoken, will help you discern your truth. Also, feel free also to discuss this exercise with your spiritual companion or mentor.

DAY TWO

Spiritual Exercise for Day True Heart Time
Gospel of Mark Chapter One:

The Cure of a Demoniac
Then they came to Capernaum, and on the Sabbath he entered the synagogue and taught. The people were astonished at his teaching, for he taught them as one having authority and not as the scribes.

In their synagogue was a man with an unclean spirit; he cried out, "What have you to do with us, Jesus of Nazareth? Have you come to destroy us? I know who you are—the Holy One of God!"

Jesus rebuked him and said, "Quiet! Come out of him!" The unclean spirit convulsed him and with a loud cry came out of him. All were amazed and asked one another, "What is this? A new teaching with authority. He commands even the unclean spirits and they obey him." His fame spread everywhere throughout the whole region of Galilee.

Pope Francis has affirmed that Satan is a real spiritual entity who seeks the destruction of people and creation. Many of us read books like *The Lord of the Rings* because it accurately depicts a spiritual world of good and evil.

Now re-read the Gospel portion and notice how, by entering into the wilderness at the beginning of his ministry, Jesus was prepared to be victorious in this battle—that includes the in battle inside each of us.

Ask Jesus to master any evil and self-centeredness you experience in your life. Know that he has the power to help you. Say aloud, "Jesus, I trust in Your power to help me be more selfless."

Feel and think the feelings and thoughts that come to you in this exercise and write down any you wish to write down in your journal.

DAY THREE

Spiritual Exercise for Day True Heart Time
Gospel of Mark Chapter Four

Parable of the Lamp
He said to them, "Is a lamp brought in to be placed under a bushel basket or under
a bed, and not to be placed on a lampstand? For there is nothing hidden except to
be made visible; nothing is secret except to come to light. Anyone who has ears to
hear ought to hear."

In this passage can you see that Jesus has invited you to the True Heart training
because he wants the light of Christ living in you to bring hope to the world?

Read it again. Find yourself in the "them" so that now you read it this way:

He said to me, "Is a lamp brought in to be placed under a bushel basket or under
a bed, and not to be placed on a lampstand? For there is nothing hidden except to
be made visible; nothing is secret except to come to light. Anyone who has ears to
hear ought to hear."

Listen to Jesus speaking about your life as a "lamp" and tell him what kind of
light you want it to bring to your friends and the world. How is the light of

selflessness different from that of self-centeredness? Maybe let this be what you write in your journal tonight.

DAY FOUR

Spiritual Exercise for Day True Heart Time
Gospel of Mark Chapter Five

The Woman with a Hemorrhage
There was a woman afflicted with hemorrhages for twelve years. She had suffered greatly at the hands of many doctors and had spent all that she had. Yet she was not helped but only grew worse. She had heard about Jesus and came up behind him in the crowd and touched his cloak.

She said, "If I but touch his clothes, I shall be cured." Immediately her flow of blood dried up. She felt in her body that she was healed of her affliction.

Jesus, aware at once that power had gone out from him, turned around in the crowd and asked, "Who has touched my clothes?" But his disciples said to him, "You see how the crowd is pressing upon you, and yet you ask, 'Who touched me?'" And he looked around to see who had done it.

The woman, realizing what had happened to her, approached in fear and trembling. She fell down before Jesus and told him the whole truth. He said to her, "Daughter, your faith has saved you. Go in peace and be cured of your affliction.

Can you feel the wisdom of this passage? Jesus comes to anyone who will be willing to accept his healing and mercy.

Let him touch anything in your life that needs physical, emotional or spiritual healing.

Believe in his power and ask him to heal you.

Feel him touch your life and believe in him.

As you feel this power and grace, discern each part of you that needs his healing. Write down or speak aloud what patterns of self-centeredness you need Jesus to heal.

DAY FIVE

Spiritual Exercise for Day True Heart Time
Gospel of Mark Chapter Six

The Rejection at Nazareth

He departed from there and came to his native place accompanied by his disciples. When the Sabbath came he began to teach in the synagogue, and many who heard him were astonished. They said, "Where did this man get all this? What kind of wisdom has been given him? What mighty deeds are wrought by his hands! Is he not the carpenter the son of Mary, and the brother of James and Joses and Judas and Simon? And are not his sisters here with us?" They took offense at him.

Jesus said to them, "A prophet is not without honor except in his native place and among his own kin and in his own house."

So he was not able to perform any mighty deed there apart from curing a few sick people by laying his hands on them. He was amazed at their lack of faith.

In his life Jesus was rejected many times because he was true to his heart and mission. Those who fought against him did not welcome him or his mission. Did he take it personally or did he let rejection bring him closer to God?

When have you felt rejected for being true to your heart and mission in life? By whom?

Describe three incidents in the last year. Was it because you were being selfless and true to your heart and mission or were you acting on self-centeredness?

Can you pray for those who reject you?

If we approach rejection with discernment, we can see why we were rejected, get past blaming the other person, and learn from the rejection so that we become increasingly true-of-heart and more selfless. Because nurturing wounds makes us more self-centered.

As you preach this gospel to yourself, in your heart, listen for Jesus' voice preaching to you. Let his gospel make you stronger, more loving, selfless and wiser young adult.

DAY SIX

Spiritual Exercise for Day True Heart Time
The Gospel of Mark Chapter Eight

The Blind Man of Bethsaida
When they arrived at Bethsaida, they brought to him a blind man and begged him
to touch him. He took the blind man by the hand and led him outside the village.
Putting spittle on his eyes he laid his hands on him and asked, "Do you see
anything?" Looking up he replied, "I see people looking like trees and walking."
Then he laid hands on his eyes a second time and he saw clearly; his sight was
restored and he could see everything distinctly. Then he sent him home and said,
"Do not even go into the village."

Reflection:
Can you feel in this passage the greatness of the revelation that Jesus is Lord of
all creation?

Imagine the passage with you as the blind person. You are not physically blind
but feel blind to important things in life about selflessness and self-centeredness
that you can't clearly see.

What are the self-centered patterns that you are blind to but want to see more
clearly?

Ask Jesus to lay his hands on the eyes of your heart to feel his press upon your real heart.

Tell him aloud you believe he can help you see and thank him for hearing your request for sight.

DAY SEVEN

Spiritual Exercise for Day True Heart Time
Gospel of Mark Chapter Eight

Peter's Confession about Jesus

Now Jesus and his disciples set out for the villages of Caesarea Philippi. Along the way he asked his disciples, "Who do people say that I am?" They said in reply, "John the Baptist, others Elijah, still others one of the prophets." And he asked them, "But who do you say that I am?" Peter said to him in reply, "You are the Messiah." Then he warned them not to tell anyone about him.

Reflection:

What thoughts and feelings arise for you in reading this passage? Ponder them.

Then re-imagine the passage taking place with a large crowd of people that you know and who know you. See Jesus come up to you and ask you to say in front of the crowd who he is.

What would you say about Jesus in front of your friends and how do you think they would react?

Play it out like a movie in your imagination but notice your thoughts, the thoughts and reactions of others and the reaction of Jesus to your statement about him.

Night Vigil Week 2

TEMPTATION IN THE WILDERNESS

Temptation in the Wilderness by John St. John Long, 2814 Photo ©Tate
https://www.tate.org.uk/art/artworks/long-the-temptation-in-the-wilderness-t04169

Do only one section at a time. Do not read ahead but stay with each section until you feel inclined to move on. Spend 15-45 minutes on this meditation

I. Gather in what your senses are experiencing. Breathe in the Spirit of God. Breathe out whatever is troubling, distracting, or burdensome. Be aware of all the thoughts and feelings coming from the day so far.

II. Talk to Jesus in your own words about your desire for this particular grace: "that I may come to know and believe God the Father as the source of my greatest freedom in being selfless and that I may come to understand more clearly the source of my greatest un-freedom in being self-centered. Stay with this for as long as you like. Don't feel compelled to move on unless your heart suggests.

III. Imagine yourself accompanying Jesus away from the Jordan River, out into the wilderness. This is the first time you have decided to go away, apart from your family and friends. This is your first attempt to spend such a lengthy time in prayer and silence with your God. You are both filled with the Holy Spirit -- yet it is not long before you are faced with the insidious seduction of the spirit of evil and darkness. See and experience the events as they happen. Notice everything about what is happening to Jesus and yourself. Do not move to the next section unless your heart suggests.

Open your Bible and enter the scene of the story in Luke 4: 1-13 See, feel, touch, and smell everything about the story because Scripture is a "living word."

IV. ASK THE LORD FOR HIS STRENGTH AND GUIDANCE in facing the temptations and the ways your spirit is not free to be a True Heart. Specifically, for the:

THE BREAD which represents the material possessions and comforts that you feel you need for status and security;

THE POWER of independence, self-sufficiency and pride which keep you, not God, as the center of your life, for not realizing your need for God as the source of your freedom and life;

THE VANITY of self-centeredness which subtly manipulates or exploits others;

ASK THE LORD FOR HIS HELP in letting go of what binds you; of what keeps you trapped in self-centeredness, from freely loving others, from freely giving your heart to God, and from freely being your truest self.

V. Following the meditation, bring your own prayer period to a close by slowly praying the *Our Father,* listening to the words in your heart as you pray.

First Colloquy, or conversation, will be with Mary. Speak with Mary, using your own words, asking her to obtain from her Son the grace to surrender comfort, self-sufficiency and self-centeredness and to be open to the Spirit working inside you. When you finish this conversation, pray the *Hail Mary* slowly, thinking of the words and the person to whom you are praying.

> *Hail Mary, full of grace The Lord is with thee.*
> *Blessed art thou amongst women*
> *and blessed is the fruit of thy womb, Jesus.*
> *Holy Mary, Mother of God, Pray for us sinners,*
> *Now and at the hour of our death.*

> *Amen.*

Second Colloquy, or conversation, will be with Jesus. Speak directly to Jesus, asking him to request his Father for the same graces as above. When you finish your conversation, pray the *Anima Christi* slowly, thinking of the words and the person to whom you are praying.

> *Soul of Christ, sanctify me. Body of Christ, save me.*
> *Blood of Christ, fill me. Water from the side of Christ wash me.*
> *Passion of Christ, strengthen me. O Good Jesus, hear me.*
> *Within thy wounds, hide me. Permit me not to be separated from thee.*
> *From the wicked foe, defend me. At the hour of my death, call me,*
> *And bid me come to thee that with thy saints*
> *I may praise thee forever and ever.*

> *Amen.*

Third Colloquy, or conversation, will be with God the Father. Ask the Father directly in your own words to give you the graces as described above. When you finish, pray the *Our Father*, thinking of the words and the person to whom you are praying.

Our Father, Who art in heaven Hallowed be thy name.
Thy Kingdom come. Thy will be done,
On earth as it is in heaven.
Give us this day our daily bread,
And forgive us our trespasses,
As we forgive those who trespass against us.
Lead us not into temptation,
But deliver us from evil.

Amen.

WEEK 3
DAY ONE

Spiritual Exercise for Day True Heart Time
Gospel of Mark Chapter Eight

Open your heart to The Gospel Story of the One who holds you and all creation in being. Jesus is real and wants to become part of your daily life. He wants a relationship with you. He waits to be your hope, your forgiveness and your peace. Ask the Holy Spirit open your heart to Jesus' story which is The Word of God

The Conditions of Discipleship
He summoned the crowd with his disciples and said to them, "Whoever wishes to come after me must deny himself, take up his cross, and follow me. For whoever wishes to save his life will lose it, but whoever loses his life for my sake and that of the gospel will save it.

What profit is there for one to gain the whole world and forfeit his life? What could one give in exchange for his life? Whoever is ashamed of me and of my words in this faithless and sinful generation, the Son of Man will be ashamed of when he comes in his Father's glory with the holy angels."

Reflection:

As you reflect on this passage, see Jesus come up to you and ask if you will follow him.

Tell him the one self-centered thing you think you must deny to freely follow him.

Tell him what you think the cross is in your life that you must selflessly carry to be his follower.

DAY TWO

Spiritual Exercise for Day True Heart Time
Gospel of Mark Chapter Nine

The Transfiguration of Jesus
After six days Jesus took Peter, James, and John and led them up a high mountain
apart by themselves. He was transfigured before them, and his clothes became
dazzling white, such as no fuller on earth could bleach them. Then Elijah appeared
to them along with Moses, and they were conversing with Jesus.

Then Peter said to Jesus in reply, "Rabbi, it is good that we are here! Let us make
three tents: one for you, one for Moses, and one for Elijah." He hardly knew what
to say, they were so terrified. Then a cloud came, casting a shadow over then\m
from the cloud came a voice, "This is my beloved Son. Listen to him."

Reflection:
The story of the transfiguration of Jesus and the glory revealed is a sign of the
coming resurrection when Christ's glory will transform "transfigure" all
creation and us as well. Can you feel this eventuality in your heart? It will be the
final victory of selflessness over self-centeredness.

Stand with Jesus and hear the Father say it about you: "This is my beloved child."
Can you hear and feel your Father's love?

What self-centeredness in your life do you want the Father to "transfigure" so that you can be a more selfless True Heart?

Be specific and ask for the grace to be beautifully transformed. Write in your journal what you desire to be transformed.

DAY THREE

Spiritual Exercise for Day True Heart Time
Gospel of Mark Chapter Nine

Temptations to Sin

"Whoever causes one of these little ones who believe [in me] to sin, it would be better for him if a great millstone were put around his neck and he were thrown into the sea. "If your hand causes you to sin, cut it off. It is better for you to enter into life maimed than with two hands to go into Gehenna, into the unquenchable fire. "And if your foot causes you to sin, cut it off. It is better for you to enter into life crippled than with two feet to be thrown into Gehenna. "And if your eye causes you to sin, pluck it out. Better for you to enter into the kingdom of God with one eye than with two eyes to be thrown into Gehenna, where 'their worm does not die, and the fire is not quenched.'

Reflection:

Jesus uses exaggeration to make a point. He is not really suggesting one cut off their body parts. But he is making the point that sin is destructive and we must fight it with discipline and his grace.

Imagine Jesus coming up to you and asking what self-centered behavior you need "cut out of your heart and life" so that you have the freedom to selflessly follow him. Remember as you ask that you can't do this, but He can.

Ask these questions of Jesus until you have listed for him everything that needs to be cut, plucked out, and changed in your life. Ask for his help and believe he has the power to change you! Write in your journal what you asked Jesus to cut out of your heart.

DAY FOUR

Spiritual Exercise for Day True Heart Time
Gospel of Mark Chapter Eleven

The Authority of Jesus Questioned

They returned once more to Jerusalem. As he was walking in the temple area, the chief priests, the scribes, and the elders approached him and said to him, "By what authority are you doing these things? Or who gave you this authority to do them?" Jesus said to them, "I shall ask you one question. Answer me, and I will tell you by what authority I do these things. Was John's baptism of heavenly or of human origin? Answer me."

They discussed this among themselves and said, "If we say, 'Of heavenly origin,' he will say, '[Then] why did you not believe him?' But shall we say, 'Of human origin'?"—they feared the crowd, for they all thought John really was a prophet. So they said to Jesus in reply, "We do not know."

Then Jesus said to them, "Neither shall I tell you by what authority I do these things."

Reflection:

Jesus is the son of the Eternal Father. Yet, the religious authorities of his time saw him as being possessed by an evil spirit and they refuse to respect his authority. The most selfless person to have ever lived is accused of being the very embodiment of self-centeredness. As he faces these misconceptions, Jesus is the model of both the courage and humility that real strength and authority are. Have you ever stood by Gospel values and had people challenge why you believe something? Has it created fear in your heart?

Remember one occasion when you stood your ground and one occasion when you caved in to the pressure of others. What can you learn from these two experiences? Write a sentence below or in your journal.

Ask Jesus to be a selfless True Heart, strong and courageous in the face of outside pressures.

DAY FIVE

Parable of the Tenants
He began to speak to them in parables.
"A man planted a vineyard, put a hedge around it, dug a wine press, and built a
tower. Then he leased it to tenant farmers and left on a journey.

"At the proper time he sent a servant to the tenants to obtain from them some of
the produce of the vineyard. But they seized him, beat him, and sent him away
empty-handed. Again he sent them another servant. And that one they beat over
the head and treated shamefully. He sent yet another whom they killed.

"So, too, many others; some they beat, others they killed until he had only one
other to send, a beloved son. He sent him to them last of all, thinking, 'They will
respect my son.' "But those tenants said to one another, 'This is the heir. Come,
let us kill him, and the inheritance will be ours.' So they seized him and killed him,
and threw him out of the vineyard.

"What [then] will the owner of the vineyard do? He will come, put the tenants to
death, and give the vineyard to others. "Have you not read this scripture passage:

'The stone that the builders rejected has become the cornerstone; by the Lord has this been done, and it is wonderful in our eyes'?"

"They were seeking to arrest him, but they feared the crowd, for they realized that he had addressed the parable to them. So they left him and went away."

Reflection:
The Good News of the Gospel proclaimed by Jesus is constantly getting him in trouble with the religious authorities. He tells these authorities a parable about how the prophets of the Old Testament were beaten or killed by their ancestors. Upon hearing the parable they wanted to arrest Jesus on the spot, but they were afraid.

What modern-day selfless prophets do you see in your country or the world who are putting their lives at risk to proclaim the Gospel? What are they proclaiming and how is the message being received?

Can you imagine selflessly standing up for something that would bring you the same condemnation? What in your life do you need to sacrifice to stand with Christ as a modern-day prophet? Write it down in your journal.

Say in your heart, "Be not afraid." Say these words when confronted by situations that call you to selflessly take a stand for the Gospel.

DAY SIX

Spiritual Exercise for Day True Heart Time
The Gospel of Mark Chapter Twelve

The Greatest Commandment
One of the scribes, when he came forward and heard them disputing and saw how well he had answered them, asked him, "Which is the first of all the commandments?"

Jesus replied, "The first is this: 'Hear, O Israel! The Lord our God is Lord alone! You shall love the Lord your God with all your heart, with all your soul, with all your mind, and with all your strength.'

The second is this: 'You shall love your neighbor as yourself.' There is no other commandment greater than these."

The scribe said to him, "Well said, teacher. You are right in saying, 'He is One and there is no other than he.' And 'to love him with all your heart, with all your understanding, with all your strength, and to love your neighbor as yourself' is worth more than all burnt offerings and sacrifices."

And when Jesus saw that [he] answered with understanding, he said to him, "You are not far from the kingdom of God." And no one dared to ask him any more questions."

Reflection:

The Greatest Commandment Jesus repeats is something every Jew would know. It is central to the Torah; *Sh'ma Yisrael Adonai Eloheinu Adonai Eḥad - "Hear, O Israel: the LORD is our God, the LORD is One."*

As a Jew and a prophet, Jesus connects this Commandment with a second Commandment that must be in place if one really says "I love God": loving one's neighbor as oneself. To love God and to love others moves us from self-centeredness to selflessness.

Can you remember an experience in your life where you felt a real love of God or another person that let you feel the joy of selflessness?

Remember it and write a single sentence below or in your journal.

Can you remember a time when selflessly "loving your neighbor" who might have been very self-centered was difficult for you? Write this person or group down and write or speak aloud why it was or is hard for you to love them.

As you reflect, ask God for strength of heart to love others more selflessly as he loves them. God loves everyone, even if they disappoint me or are self-centered. That is a great truth Jesus taught us.

DAY SEVEN

Spiritual Exercise for Day True Heart Time
Gospel of Mark Chapter Twelve

The Poor Widow's Contribution
He sat down opposite the treasury and observed how the crowd put money into the treasury. Many rich people put in large sums. A poor widow also came and put in two small coins worth a few cents.

Calling his disciples, he said to them, "Amen, I say to you, this poor widow put in more than all the other contributors to the treasury. For they have all contributed from their surplus wealth, but she, from her poverty, has contributed all she had, her whole livelihood."

Reflection:
Take a moment to think of those who have made the greatest selfless sacrifices in life for you. It might appear as if they have done almost nothing, but they have done a lot, haven't they?

Why did it look like no real selfless sacrifice was being made by this parent, mentor, or friend?

Can it be that your discernment process was not well established so you missed how deeply this person was sacrificing selflessly for you?

What is the greatest selfless sacrifice you have made in your life?

Have others seen it? Has that sacrifice been invisible to them?

If you were to selflessly give up your whole livelihood like this woman, what would you put in that collection basket? Write it down in your journal.

NIGHT VIGIL WEEK 3

JESUS ACCUSED OF BEING THE DEVIL

Christ and the Pharisees by Ernst Karl Zimmermann

Do only one section at a time. Do not read ahead but stay with each section until you feel inclined to move on. Spend 15-45 minutes on this meditation.

I. Begin this meditation by asking Jesus to be with you. Ask Jesus to give you the graces he feels will be best for you during this time of the night vigil and this time of training. Specifically, ask for the grace to know how the religious leaders of Jesus' day could have mistaken him and his message as satanic. Pray to understand how the values of Jesus can be seen as evil and hateful in our own time. Use the *Triple Colloquy* below to ask for these graces.

II. Open your Bible to the twelfth chapter of Matthew, verses twenty-two to thirty-two. Before you read, plan to read it slowly so you can visualize the scenes as they really happened; only place yourself in the scene to see and feel the profound tensions between Jesus and the religious leaders. Notice all the details of the people, the smells, the sounds, etc. Keep aware of all the thoughts and feelings you had entering this meditation; only now let yourself be distracted by the events as they unfold before you.

Watch Jesus perform his act of curing the possessed man, restoring his sight and hearing. How does the crowd react? How does the man cured thank Jesus? Why are the religious leaders so angered by Jesus' act of mercy? What are the tensions you feel in the crowd between Jesus, his followers and those denouncing him? How do the leaders react when Jesus speaks to them about blasphemy against the Holy Spirit?

III. Pay attention to your reaction to the events that have unfolded before you. See the man leave the presence of Jesus. Walk up to Jesus from your place in the crowd. You are present before Jesus so no one else in the crowd can hear you. Speak to Jesus about what you have just seen and heard. What do you say? What does he say? What invitation does he extend to you?

IV. Ask Jesus if there is anything you have confused as evil or hateful that is actually holy and good. Tell him why you are confused. What does he tell you? What do you say in return? What is Jesus' response? Stop and listen. What are you thinking and feeling?

V. Pray: *Take, Lord, and receive all my liberty, my memory, my understanding, and my entire will; all that I have and possess. You have given all to me. To you, Lord, I return it. Everything is yours; dispose of it according to your will. Give me only your love and your grace. That is enough for me. Amen!*

First Colloquy, or conversation, will be with Mary. Speak with Mary, using your own words asking her to obtain from her Son the grace to follow her Son selflessly in every act and decision of your life. When you finish this conversation, pray the *Hail Mary* slowly, thinking of the words and the person to whom you are praying.

Hail Mary, full of grace The Lord is with thee.
Blessed art thou amongst women
and blessed is the fruit of thy womb, Jesus.
Holy Mary, Mother of God, Pray for us sinners,
Now and at the hour of our death.

Amen.

Second Colloquy, or conversation, will be with Jesus. Speak directly to Jesus, asking him to request his Father for the same graces as above, i.e., that you may selflessly follow Jesus. When you finish your conversation, pray the *Anima Christi* slowly, thinking of the words and the person to whom you are praying.

Soul of Christ, sanctify me. Body of Christ, save me.
Blood of Christ, fill me. Water from the side of Christ wash me.
Passion of Christ, strengthen me. O Good Jesus, hear me.
Within thy wounds, hide me. Permit me not to be separated from thee.
From the wicked foe, defend me. At the hour of my death, call me,
And bid me come to thee that with thy saints
I may praise thee forever and ever.

Amen.

Third Colloquy, or conversation, will be with God the Father. Ask the Father directly in your own words to give you the graces so you may selflessly follow His Son. When you finish, pray the *Our Father,* thinking of the words and the person to whom you are praying.

Our Father, Who art in heaven Hallowed be thy name.
Thy Kingdom come. Thy will be done,
On earth as it is in heaven.
Give us this day our daily bread,
And forgive us our trespasses,
As we forgive those who trespass against us.
Lead us not into temptation,
But deliver us from evil.

Amen.

WEEK 4

DAY ONE

Spiritual Exercise for Day True Heart Time

In the previous two weeks, you followed Jesus' story in Mark's Gospel. Today during one of your True Heart periods, ask for Spirit's inspiration to move you deeper into Jesus' story as it connects to your own life story.

To help you in this task, ask in words *from your TRUE HEART,* to discover or remember the most intimate and/or meaningful name for God the Father, Son and Spirit that you have used in prayer. That name will resonate deeply in your heart and reflect God's relationship to you and your personal relationship with God. Ask for the grace to discover the name for God that touches your heart most intimately unlocking your selflessness and neutralizing your self-centeredness.

You will know the right name because it has the power to unlock your trust, love and to stir your affections.

The following names may help you in your discovery:

Merciful Father, Loving Father, Almighty Father, Our Father, Father God, Loving Creator, Creator God, God of Love, My God, Holy God, Father of the

Poor, God of All Mercy, God of All Compassion, Father of Jesus, Lord Jesus Christ, Lord Jesus, Christ Jesus, Dear Jesus, Adorable Jesus, Adorable Christ, Good Jesus, Jesus, Merciful Savior, Jesus My Savior, Son of God, Dearest Lord, My Lord, My Lord and My God, Sacred Heart of Jesus, Lamb of God, Good Shepherd, Crucified Savior, Holy Spirit, Spirit of Jesus, Spirit of the Lord, Loving Spirit, Holy Spirit of God, Love of God, Divine Spirit, Creator Spirit, Creator God.

Write the name for God in your notebook when you discover it. From this point forward, use this name when you address God.

God delights when you use a personal name and speak directly from your heart.

A suggestion: Use this name to address God every time you naturally think of God throughout the day. For example, you may say in your heart before a meeting: "Lord Jesus, be with me now." Say it, and then just move on with your meeting. Do not make this a tedious exercise, but one that feels natural and relaxed. You do not have to think long and hard about God. The purpose of this spontaneous prayer is just a short, friendly reminder of God's presence and love for you. Use this name in all your True Heart exercises and prayers from this day forward.

DAY TWO

Spiritual Exercise for Day True Heart Time

All the remaining spiritual exercises for weeks four to six are to help you "see" your life history in light of the opposing values of selflessness and self-centeredness. You will then have the opportunity and grace to make a Whole-Life Confession. God is with you. Be Not Afraid!

Each of us has persons, issues and life events that shape our life story, our history. These persons, life events and issues are linked to the spiritual plotlines in our life story, leading towards or away from God—towards selflessness or self-centeredness.

We are conscious of some of these persons, issues and events but others are buried deep in our memory. Because these significant elements often evade our conscious awareness, we need to rely on God's grace to reveal them. We ask for grace to understand those things that, in negative and positive ways, most strongly shape us.

Today we seek God's grace to awaken to our *affective memories*. That is, we want to recall the persons, life events or issues, and *feel* the emotional weight, and the heart-value they have in our history. Seek insight into the closest, most intimate circle of people and events in your life story—parents, family, friends, and important events. Try to be attentive to the feeling these memories evoke.

For one life event, I might feel fear (something that has the power to generate the anxiety I know as fear). For another life event, my predominant feeling might be anger (someone or something that hurt me or a loved one).

For one person, I might feel mostly love (someone who has cared deeply for me). For another person, I might feel anger (someone who hurt me in some way). For one issue, my predominant feeling might be grief (the loss of a loved one or an opportunity that grieves my heart). For another issue, my experience might be gratitude or hope (an issue that has positively transformed my life for the better).

Pray that God enlighten your mind and heart to know each person, issue or life event and the *single, predominant* feeling (fear, anger, grief or self-centeredness—gratitude, hope, love or selflessness) each inspires. Take some time today to write below the three that most readily come to heart.

As you become aware of each, pause briefly and write down the name of the person, or the issue or life event that comes to memory. Next to each of these, write a *single* word for the most predominant *feeling* that arises in your heart. A word of caution here: do not succumb to the temptation to analyze or judge the feelings as they arise.

THREE PERSONS/LIFE EVENTS/ISSUES THAT GENERATE
GRATITUDE, HOPE, LOVE & SELFLESSNESS

Persons/Life Events/Issues   *Gratitude/Hope/Love/Selflessness*

1.   1.

2.   2.

3.   3.

THREE PERSONS/LIFE EVENTS/ISSUES THAT GENERATE
FEAR, ANGER, GRIEF & SELF-CENTEREDNESS

Persons/Life Events/Issues   *Fear/Anger/Grief /Self-Centeredness*

1.   1.

2.   2.

3.   3.

DAY THREE

Spiritual Exercise for Day True Heart Time

Over the next days we will review the Decalogue known as the Ten Commandments, in order to help you to better understand your life story and the gift of healing, balance and selflessness that God desires for you.

Use your personal name for God and pray that your imagination be illumined so that the *most important* issues in the Commandments, those that illuminate your history in both its selflessness and self-centeredness, will come into your mind and heart.

Pray to "see" what you have *never* seen before. Pray to see your life as God sees your life.

Read these words and hold them to you as you prepare for a reflection on these "laws of right-relationship."[13]

---

[13] "The Commandments were given to the Chosen People in a Covenant that was sealed with a blood sacrifice. The Church reflects that the power of the animal sacrifice sealing the Covenant receives its power from Christ's blood, which it foreshadows. The Commandments, as *gift*, are a foundation for God's work to repair our broken self-centered human nature, to forgive us, and reopen the way to eternity through selfless thoughts, words and deeds: the work of Christ's death and resurrection. It is no wonder then that laws enshrining the Commandments' truths have

For this exercise, you will reflect on the Commandments to enhance your understanding of their richness and wisdom. The exercise will help to clarify how each Commandment carries its own responsibilities and boundaries for *you*. These *Decrees*—a synonym for *Commandments*— will ignite your imagination so you may be able to hear them differently now than ever before.

The ten decrees serve as a reminder to us when we have forgotten to *remember and know the truth* about God, humanity and ourselves. They are a *gift* to guide our way home so our thoughts, words and deeds bring selflessness and life, not self-centeredness and death.

Before concluding your prayer period today, use your notebook to record where in your life you have missed the mark in living the Decree you reflected on. Be specific, honest and courageous. Ask for the grace of integrity and openness to embrace the truth of your own experience.

A helpful format to follow as you reflect on each Decree is this one: Identify the Decree (and the sub-themes in the Decrees) as mild, moderate, or strong depending on the challenge this specific Decree presents to you.

For example, in this format, you might write:

"6th—moderate, especially regarding (put your issue in this parenthesis);"

"4th—mild regarding (put the person here);"

"7th/10th—strong regarding (place the event here)."

---

transformed stories of self-centeredness and injustice to stories of selflessness and justice for countless millions of people in the last three millennia."

Use codes, if you prefer, to safeguard confidentiality. By protecting confidentiality you can be fully honest without worrying about hurting someone should your journal get read in the future by someone other than you.

Note: The purpose of this exercise is to simply identify your challenges with the Commandments. With Christ by your side, explore this exercise with curiosity and detachment, without self-blame. God sees beyond any patterns of sin and failure you have or think you have. God knows *you* for who you are. God loves you.

God is the Divine Physician who desires to help you honestly see your life as it is so that He can bring forgiveness, healing, freedom selflessness and peace into you.

First Decree: I am the Lord your God,
you shall have no strange gods before me.

Ask yourself some sacred questions:

Is God the center of my life?

Have I displaced God with my studies, technologies, or concern for wealth and pleasure?

Does the worship and honor of God take shape in my weekly religious practices? Do I pray often?

Do I turn to God for forgiveness often?

Have I resorted to relying on superstition, the occult or astrology in place of asking for God's assistance?

*Second Decree: You shall not take
the name of the Lord your God in vain.*

Ask yourself some important questions:

Do I casually take God's name in vain?

Do I have a habit of swearing in jest or in anger?

Do I use God's name to damn other people?

Do I nurse hatred of God in my heart?

Do I harbor anger towards God for the difficult things in my life or in the world?

Do I revere God in my heart?

As you feel moved, write brief answers here or in your journal.

If you see that you are unfaithful to these decrees, how can you institute change in your life right now? Be inspired! Be a True Heart! Be Selfless!

DAY FOUR

Spiritual Exercise for Day True Heart Time

Today you will reflect again on the Commandments in order to enhance your understanding of their richness and wisdom in *your* life. This exercise will help to clarify how each Commandment carries its own responsibilities and boundaries.

Remember, the idea here is to look at these *Decrees*—a synonym for *Commandments*—in a way that will ignite your imagination so that you will be able to hear them differently today than before. These decrees—statements by God--are a *gift* to guide our way home.

Before concluding your prayer period today, use your notebook to record where in your life you have missed the mark in living the Decree you reflected on. Be specific, honest and courageous. Ask for the grace of integrity and openness to embrace the truth of your own experience.

Remember, follow the format for identifying issues you learned yesterday.

Third Decree: Remember to keep holy the Sabbath day.

Ask yourself some life-changing questions:

Do I make every effort to prepare myself for the Sunday Liturgy?

Do I make every effort to attend the Sunday Liturgy?

Do I allow social or sporting events to displace or limit my attendance at the Sunday Liturgy?

Do I limit unnecessary servile work on Sunday?

Is Sunday a true day of spiritual rest and refreshment?

Fourth Decree: Honor your Father and Mother.

Ask yourself some key family questions:

Do I give proper reverence to my mom and dad for the gift of life?

Do I thank them?

Do I spend time with them?

Do I strive to forgive the shortcomings of my parents?

Do I hold anger or grudges against them in my heart?

Do I try to respond to them with love and charity?

Do I attend to them in their sufferings and weaknesses?

Am I patient with their infirmity as they age?

As you feel moved, write brief answers here or in your journal.

If you see that you are unfaithful to these decrees, how can you institute change in your life right now? Be inspired! Be a True Heart! Be Selfless!

DAY FIVE

Spiritual Exercise for Day True Heart Time

It is time again to reflect on the Commandments. Before concluding your prayer period, use your notebook to record where in your life you have missed the mark in living the Decrees you reflected on. Be specific, honest and courageous. Ask for the grace of integrity and openness to embrace the truth of your own experience.

Fifth Decree: You shall not kill.

Ask yourself critical life questions:

Do I strive to overcome the prejudices I have against individuals or groups?

Do I resist acting on my prejudices so as not to harm persons with my words or deeds?

Do I act with cruelty toward others?

Do I risk my life or the lives of others by using illegal drugs?

Do I risk my life or the lives of others by driving recklessly or intoxicated?

Do I strive in words and deeds to promote the value of life from conception to natural death?

Have I ever helped someone terminate a pregnancy or end his/her own life?

Do I strive to do everything I can to uphold the value of each person?

Do I harbor satisfaction in my heart at the death of those people whom I consider evil?

Do I vote for politicians/civil servants because of their positions to protect and promote abortion, euthanasia, capital punishment or pre-emptive war?

Do I mourn the loss of all human life, no matter the cause of death?

Sixth Decree: You shall not commit adultery.
Ninth Decree: You shall not covet your neighbor's spouse.

Ask yourself some critical relationship questions: By how I live now, how will I protect my potential future covenant relationship with my spouse and uphold its sacredness?

By how I live now, how will I uphold my covenant by never engaging in any sexual activity with someone other than my spouse?

By how I live now, how will I protect my imagination from pornography's capacity to distort my image of women or men?

How will I strive to cultivate purity of heart as a sign of God's own single-heartedness?

How will I reverence sexual intercourse first and foremost as a gift of love to create a human life destined for an eternity with God?

As you feel moved, write answers in your journal. Conclude your Night Vigil by writing one or two sentences on what you would like the biography of your life to say regarding the sacredness with which you *live out the gift* of your human sexuality.[14]

---

[14] For challenges with unwanted sexual behaviors like sexting, masturbation and pornography, visit RECLAiM at www.ReclaimSexualHealth.com They are a Catholic web-based, inexpensive and anonymous program that use the latest in brain science to help people of all ages overcome unwanted sexual habits and find peace, hope and true relationships: "Mending Minds-Saving Souls-Healing Hearts."

DAY SIX

Spiritual Exercise for Day True Heart Time

It is time again to reflect on the Commandments. Before concluding your prayer period, use your notebook to record where in your life you have missed the mark in living the Decrees you reflected on. Be specific, honest and courageous. Ask for the grace of integrity and openness to embrace the truth of your own experience.

Seventh Decree: You shall not steal.
Tenth Decree: You shall not covet your neighbor's goods.

Ask yourself some important character questions:

Do I cheat to get ahead?

Do I take things that do not belong to me?

Do I keep things I have borrowed?

Do I vandalize or harm property or goods that do not belong to me?

Do I envy those who have more than I do?

Do I live with envy of those who have more than I do?

Do I respect the limited resources of the earth as a divine inheritance to benefit all people?

Do I give my old items and some money to the poor?

As you feel moved, write very brief answers here or in your journal.

If you see that you are unfaithful to these decrees, how can you institute change in your life right now? Be inspired! Be a True Heart! Be Selfless!

DAY SEVEN

Spiritual Exercise for Day True Heart Time

For this last exercise of the week, pray for the grace to remember the movie, song or novel (story) that has the power to bring you to tears.

Use your personal name for God to be graced to remember the turn of phrase, the lyric, the dialogue, the word spoken, the melody, the image that has touched your heart so profoundly that your only response was tears.

What causes us to weep holds significance in our history, and informs our life story.

Pray to remember and feel what moves you to tears.

The Gospels record that Jesus wept twice. He wept over Jerusalem, for failing to recognize that the time of its deliverance was at hand (Lk 19: 41-44). And He wept for His good friend Lazarus, "see how he loved him" (Jn 11: 33-6).

Both instances reveal Jesus' deep longing for humanity's reconciliation and peace. It is Christ's desire to bring freedom from death's grip—freedom from the death that resulted from humanity's disobedience and self-centeredness. Jesus' weeping expresses the deepest longings of His selfless heart. His tears reveal His mission in life, a mission He received from the Father, to save those He loves.

Tears reveal many of the deepest longings of our own hearts, too. They are a window to the heart and soul.

Ask God for the grace to remember and understand what brings you to tears, what breaks your heart or expresses your heart's longings for healing and peace.

Sit apart in a quiet place. Find a comfortable position that permits you to be alert. Breathe deeply for a few minutes, mindful that God's love sustains your very life.

Using your personal name for God to ask for enlightenment in your memory and imagination so that you can remember and understand what brings you to tears, and why.

How is your life-mission—your story—revealed in your tears?

What movie, song or novel (story) moved you to tears and what can God help you understand about your life from those artworks?

Before your prayer period ends, write down what caused your tears.

Record why it caused your tears, if it is clear to you.

Reflect further on what this might possibly reveal to you about your selfless True Heart.

NIGHT VIGIL WEEK 4

PEACE, BE STILL

Peace, Be Still by Arnold Friberg

Be open to all thoughts, feelings, and ideas you have coming from the day. Spend some time talking with God about the things you think significant. Stay here as long as you are comfortable. **Be Alone.**

I. Begin this meditation by asking Jesus to be with you. Ask Jesus to give you the graces he feels will be best for you during this time of the night vigil and this time of training. Specifically ask for the grace to know the good you desire and how you can be tempted to believe that Jesus is not working in you or loves you when you feel your weakness and sinfulness. Pray for the grace to know why you can feel bad when God is actually energizing your conscience to know your True Heart. Use the *Triple Colloquy* below to ask for these graces.

II. Open your Bible to the fifth chapter of Luke, verses one to eleven. Before you read, plan to read it slowly so you can visualize the scenes as they really happened; only place yourself on the boat as one of the disciples. Notice all the details of the people, the smells, the sounds, etc. Keep aware of all the thoughts and feelings you had entering this meditation; only now let yourself be distracted by the events as they unfold before you.

What is Peter's dilemma? Can you sense what he may be feeling as he speaks to Jesus and asks him to leave him? What is Jesus' response? What does Jesus offer him? Speak to Peter after he is invited by Jesus to be a fisher of people. What is his joy or confusion? What does he say?

III. Pay attention to your reaction to the events that have unfolded before you. See the man leave the presence of Jesus. Walk up to Jesus from your place in the crowd. You are present before Jesus so no one else in the crowd can hear you. Speak to Jesus about what you have just seen and heard. What do you say? What does he say?

IV. Ask Jesus if there is anything in your own life that would prevent you from being a disciple of his. Ask Jesus about any particular things in your own life that cause you shame and make you think Jesus could not or does not love you. What do you say? What is Jesus' response? Stop and listen. What are you thinking and feeling?

V. Pray: *Take, Lord, and receive all my liberty, my memory, my understanding, and my entire will; all that I have and possess. You have given all to me. To you, Lord, I return it. Everything is yours; dispose of it according to your will. Give me only your love and your grace. That is enough for me. Amen!*

TRIPLE COLLOQUY OF SAINT IGNATIUS

First Colloquy, or conversation, will be with Mary. Speak with Mary, using your own words asking her to obtain from her Son the grace to follow her Son selflessly in every act and decision of your life. When you finish this conversation, pray the *Hail Mary* slowly, thinking of the words and the person to whom you are praying.

> *Hail Mary, full of grace The Lord is with thee.*
> *Blessed art thou amongst women*
> *and blessed is the fruit of thy womb, Jesus.*
> *Holy Mary, Mother of God, Pray for us sinners,*
> *Now and at the hour of our death.*

> *Amen.*

Second Colloquy, or conversation, will be with Jesus. Speak directly to Jesus, asking him to request his Father for the same graces as above, i.e., that you may follow Jesus selflessly. When you finish your conversation, pray the *Anima Christi* slowly, thinking of the words and the person to whom you are praying.

> *Soul of Christ, sanctify me. Body of Christ, save me.*
> *Blood of Christ, fill me. Water from the side of Christ wash me.*
> *Passion of Christ, strengthen me. O Good Jesus, hear me.*
> *Within thy wounds, hide me. Permit me not to be separated from thee.*
> *From the wicked foe, defend me. At the hour of my death, call me,*
> *And bid me come to thee that with thy saints*
> *I may praise thee forever and ever.*

> *Amen.*

Third Colloquy, or conversation, will be with God the Father. Ask the Father directly in your own words to give you the graces so you may selflessly follow His Son. When you finish, pray the *Our Father,* thinking of the words and the person to whom you are praying.

Our Father, Who art in heaven Hallowed be thy name.
Thy Kingdom come. Thy will be done,
On earth as it is in heaven.
Give us this day our daily bread,
And forgive us our trespasses,
As we forgive those who trespass against us.
Lead us not into temptation,
But deliver us from evil.

Amen.

WEEK 5

DAY ONE

Spiritual Exercise for Day True Heart Time
The Seven Capital Vices

For Week 5, two valuable spiritual analytic trainings form most of the exercises. They focus on our vices and addictions, offering you the potential for great enlightenment about both selflessness and self-centeredness. If we seek medical advice for pain, the doctor asks us where we hurt. Christ, the Divine Physician, asks us about our vices and addictions to discover where we are hurting, and our unsuccessful attempts to anesthetize our hurt—"self" centered therapies that ultimately don't help us. The Gospel calls vices and addictions "sin" because they manifest habits that erode our true human nature and our faith, hope and love and are…well…self-centered. The doctor calls them destructive because they ruin our lives and relationships—our selflessness, joy and peace.

In the series of training exercises this week, you'll pay attention to your vices (Pride, Gluttony, Lust, Sloth, Envy, Avarice, & Anger). They are sometimes called capital sins (from *caput*, the Latin word for *head*) because they are root habits or vices that lead to our problems of self-centeredness. All of us are subject to vices that have the ability to hook us mildly, moderately or strongly.

As you work this week, you will gradually identify your capital sins/vices. As you do this work, ask Christ, the Divine Physician, to help you understand their *source* and *context* in *your* life history.

If you can honestly identify addictions and vices in your life, you are on a path to selflessness. If you pray to Christ, the Divine Physician, *to wake you up* to the *connections* between them in your life story, you can rejoice because your healing—the healing that leads to selfless freedom--will now begin.

Remember: Christ came to save self-centered sinners, not the righteous. *TRUE HEART* is *about allowing Christ to help us identify* where we need His healing graces to overcome our self-centeredness. This is the great gift He wants to give to us. Be not afraid. Christ knows you are working with him to minimize self-centeredness and maximize selflessness.

So, use your personal name for God to pray with words from your heart that will enable you to see what you have not seen before *and* to see connections between aspects of your life story.

At the end of each prayer period mark down in your notebook all the capital vices that trap you and to which you are susceptible. Be brief in your writing, but specific. List how the capital sins/vices of Pride and Greed ensnare you and how intensely (mildly, moderately or strongly) they ensnare you in self-centeredness.

Ask for the grace of deeper understanding, and with Christ, observe your life with compassionate curiosity, and with objectivity. God sees beyond any vices you have or think you have. God knows you for who you are and loves you.

After reading about pride and greed, write in your notebook briefly and specifically: list the capital sins/vices that ensnare you and how intensely (mildly, moderately or strongly) they ensnare you in self-centered behavior.

PRIDE

Pride is an unrestrained and improper appreciation of our own worth. This is listed first because it is widely considered the most serious of the seven sins. A more modern word for pride is narcissism. This pride, this narcissism, was Adam and Eve's sinful fall into the serpent's temptation "to be like gods." Adam and Eve displaced God, the Creator, and made themselves the "center" of the world—self-centered. Their action led to the loss of paradise and to a world of sickness, self-centeredness and death.

Pride often leads to the committing of other capital sins. It is manifest in our lives as vanity and narcissism about our appearance, intelligence, status, wealth, clichés, connections, power, successes and all the other things that we use to stand apart from others and from God.

HUMILITY works against pride by removing one's ego and boastfulness, therefore allowing the attitude of service.

JOURNAL: In your journal, write very briefly one or two ways you see at this point in your life how pride (narcissism) manifests making you self-centered.

GREED

Greed is also known as avarice or covetousness. It is the immoderate desire for earthly goods and power. It is a sin of excess. Yet the object of our greed need not be evil. The problem lies in the way a person regards or desires an object, making it a god and investing it with false value.

Money can be that object as greed for money can inspire sinful actions such as hoarding, theft, fraud, environmental waste, cheating or lying.

CHARITY or love works against greed by putting the desire to help others above storing up treasure for one's self.

JOURNAL: In your journal, write very briefly one or two ways you see at this point in your life how greed manifests making your self-centered

JOURNAL NOTES

DAY TWO

Spiritual Exercise for Day True Heart Time
The Seven Capital Vices

This week you are paying attention to the vices (Pride, Gluttony, Lust, Sloth, Envy, Avarice, & Anger). All of us are subject to vices that have the ability to hook us mildly, moderately or strongly.

After reading about gluttony, lust and sloth, write in your notebook briefly and specifically: list the capital sins/vices that ensnare you and how intensely (mildly, moderately or strongly) they ensnare you in self-centered behavior.

GLUTTONY

Gluttony comes from the Latin word meaning to gulp down or swallow. It is the sin of over-indulgence and usually refers to over-consumption of food and drink. Gluttony can manifest in eating too soon, too expensively, or eating too much.

St. Alphonsus Liguori explained that feeling pleasure in eating is not wrong. Because food tastes good, we are delighted by this gift. It is not right, however, to eat with self-centered pleasure as the only motive and to forget food's function in sustaining vitality and health.

TEMPERANCE works against gluttony by implanting the desire to be healthy, therefore making one fit to serve others

JOURNAL: In your journal, briefly write one way you see at this point in your life how gluttony manifests in your life as self-centeredness.

LUST

The sin of lust refers to self-centered desires of a sexual nature. Sexuality is a gift from God and pure in itself. However, lust refers to the impure thoughts and actions that misuse that gift. Lust deviates from God's law and sexuality's sacred purpose of allowing woman and man to participate in God's creative nature—God's selflessness. Lust includes actions like sex outside marriage, adultery, rape, pornography and auto-erotic behaviors.

CHASTITY or Self-control works against lust by controlling passion and leveraging that energy for the good of others

JOURNAL: In your journal, write briefly one way you see at this point in your life how lust manifests as self-centeredness.

SLOTH

Sloth is often described simply as the sin of laziness. However, while this is part of sloth's character, its true face is *spiritual* laziness. So the sin of sloth means being lazy and lax about living the Faith and practicing virtue. Paraphrasing The Catholic Encyclopedia, sloth means aversion to labor or exertion—*to spiritual training.*

As a capital or deadly vice, St. Thomas calls it sadness in the face of some spiritual good that one has to achieve. In other words, a slothful person is bothered by the effort to sustain one's friendship with God. In this sense, sloth is directly opposed to charity.

DILIGENCE or Zeal works against slothfulness by placing the best interest of others above the life of ease and relaxation.

JOURNAL: In your journal, write briefly one way you see at this point in your life how sloth manifests in your life making you self-centered.

DAY THREE

Spiritual Exercise for Day True Heart Time
The Seven Capital Vices

God sees beyond any vices you have or think you have. God knows you for who you are and loves you. Jesus, the Divine Physician, watches compassionately and carries the burden for all your vices. He desires that you gain greater understanding and freedom. He has great compassion and patience for those seeking His help and healing.

After reading about envy and anger, write in your notebook briefly and specifically: list the capital sins/vices that ensnare you and how intensely (mildly, moderately or strongly) they ensnare you in self-centered behavior. [15]

---

[15] We've chosen images of the seven deadly sins from Pieter Bruegel, the most significant artist of the Dutch and Flemish Renaissance. The engravings are troubling, as they should be. The 2019 movie, Shazam, based on a D.C. Comics hero, render the seven deadly sins as evil beings who work to destroy the earth and people.

INVIDIA HORRENDVM MONSTRVM, SÆVISSIMA PESTIS

ENVY

The sin of envy or jealousy is more than just someone wanting what others have. Sinful envy leads us to emotions or feelings of upset at another's good fortune or blessings. The law of love naturally leads us to rejoice in the good luck of one's neighbor but envy opposes love. Envy is named among the capital sins because of the other sins to which it leads.

KINDNESS works against envy by placing the desire to help others above the need to supersede them

JOURNAL: In your journal, write briefly one way you see at this point in your life how envy manifests as self-centeredness.

WRATH

Wrath or Anger may be described as excessive and powerful feelings of hatred and resentment. These feelings can manifest as a passionate denial of truths expressed by others. Anger can also manifest in the form of denying truths about one's own life and impatience with the procedure of law. Anger is manifest too, in the desire to seek revenge outside of the workings of the justice system.

Anger, in essence, is wishing to do evil or harm to others. The transgressions borne of vengeance are among the most serious, including assault, murder, and in extreme cases, genocide and other crimes against humanity. Anger is the only sin not necessarily associated with selfishness or self-interest, although one can be angry for selfish reasons, such as jealousy.

PATIENCE works against wrath by taking time to understand the needs and desires of others before acting or speaking.

JOURNAL: In your journal, write briefly one way you see at this point in your life how anger undermines your TRUE HEART and manifests as self-centeredness.

DAY FOUR

Spiritual Exercise for Day True Heart Time
A Short Introduction to Addiction

The word *addiction* is used in many contexts. Common usage of the term has evolved to include psychological dependence. In this context, the term goes beyond drug addiction and substance abuse problems to reflect behaviors that are not generally recognized by the medical community as addictive problems such as compulsive overeating or hoarding.

When the term *addiction* is applied to compulsions that are not substance-related, such as problem gambling and internet or gaming addiction, it describes a recurring compulsion one engages in despite the activity's harmful consequences to one's individual physical, mental, social or spiritual health.[16]

Other forms of addiction could be money addictions, work addiction, exercise addiction, habitual overeating, habitual shopping, sex addiction, computer addiction, e-mail addiction, pornography addiction, and television addiction.

---

[16] "Compulsion, impaired control, persistence, irritability, relapse, and craving—these are all the hallmarks of addiction—any addiction." Gabor Maté, *In the Realm of Hungry Ghosts: Close Encounters with Addiction* (Berkeley: North Atlantic Books, 2010), 136-7.

The psychologist Gabor Maté sums up addiction's profile: "Addiction is any repeated behavior, substance-related or not, in which a person feels compelled to persist, regardless of its negative impact on his life and the lives of others. Addiction involves:

a.   Compulsive engagement with a behavior, or a preoccupation with it.

b.   Impaired control over the behavior.

c.   Persistence or relapse despite evidence of harm.

d.   Dissatisfaction, irritability, or intense craving when the object—be it a drug, activity, or other goal—is not immediately available."[17]

In your journal, write down the one hope you have regarding your life and addictions and one fear you have regarding your life and addictions. We all have addictions. They are manifestations of self-centeredness.

Based on the profile provided by Maté, reflect on any addictions you find yourself living with at this point in your life. Don't judge yourself.

Jesus the Divine Physician is by your side as you write. He is present to you to help you discover anything that can be identified to help you be more of the selfless True Heart you desire.

Be not afraid! Be selfless in confronting the self-centeredness of addictive patterns![18]

---

[17] Gabor Maté, *In the Realm of Hungry Ghosts: Close Encounters with Addiction* (Berkeley: North Atlantic Books, 2010), 136-7.

[18] For challenges with unwanted sexual behaviors like sexting, masturbation and pornography, visit RECLAiM at www.ReclaimSexualHealth.com They are a Catholic, web-based, inexpensive and anonymous program that use the latest in brain science to help people of all ages overcome unwanted sexual habits and find peace, hope and true relationships: "Mending Minds-Saving Souls-Healing Hearts."

DAY FIVE

Spiritual Exercise for Day True Heart Time
Addiction as Self-Centeredness

Ignatius was addicted to gambling and possibly to sex. Everyone has addictions (whether mild moderate or strong) to one or more things. Our addictions reveal valuable analytic information about the sources of our self-centeredness and how we seek to escape the pain it causes. All this information is worth bringing to the Divine Physician.

Today sit apart in your quiet place. Find a comfortable position that permits you to be alert. Breathe deeply for a few minutes, mindful that God's love sustains your very life.

Use your personal name for God as you ask God to enlighten your memory and imagination so that you can see any addictions you have. Are you addicted to anything?

Based on the profile provided by Gabor Mate from Day Four, write down in your journal any addictions you find yourself living with at this point in your life.

As you do this training, don't judge yourself. Jesus the Divine Physician is by your side as you write. Be not afraid.

Be brief and specific. Identify each addiction by name and frequency: **Seldom**, **Often**, or **Constantly**.

For example, you might write:

Internet Gaming—S;

Exercise—O;

Pornography—O;

Food—C.

Texting—C

Seeking to become selfless involves many joys and many adaptations inside us. Hold this material about addictions near your heart as you move forward this week with your True Heart journey to selflessness. And always, be kind and patient with yourself as is the Divine Physician.

DAY SIX

Spiritual Exercise for Day True Heart Time
Seeing the Links between Vices and Addictions

For your training today, combine the spiritual diagnostics on vices and addictions into a single training exercise by praying for the grace to honestly recognize the vices and addictions manifesting self-centeredness that erode your freedom and compromise your True Heart.

To begin this training session, you can sit in your standard manner of private prayer then, during your training session, review what you wrote in your notebook and ask Christ, the Divine Physician, in very personal words, to help you discover the *connections* between the vices and addictions.

For example, you may notice that when you are angry, you might move toward one or other addictive behavior. Or when you are envious, you might be drawn to other addictive behaviors, and so on for the other vices.

The grace you are asking for today is the *inspiration* to *understand* the vices and addictions in and of themselves, and then to identify the *connections* between them as they manifest in your life story. When, through grace, you begin to wake up to the links between the thoughts, words and deeds of your life story, you will find your True Heart waiting to help you.

Before the end of your training period, after you record in your journal any discoveries you make between the vices and addictions that God reveals to you, thank God for the courage to honestly see yourself as you are.

Thank God for the grace to wake up to live in greater freedom and selflessness. And always, be patient and kind to yourself as is Christ the Divine Physician who longs for your selfless freedom.

DAY SEVEN

Spiritual Exercise for Day True Heart Time
Discovering Links Between Your Vices, The Commandments & Any Addictions

Review the vices and commandments (I've provided them here), then fill in the analytic chart below.

As you do all of this, look for Links between the vices and the commandments in your Story.

Provide *at least one element* for each of the statements.

VICES

Pride, Envy, Gluttony, Lust, Sloth, Greed, Wrath

COMMANDMENTS

First: I am the Lord your God, you shall have no strange gods before Me.

Second: You shall not take the name of the Lord your God in vain.

Third:	Remember to keep holy the Sabbath day.
Fourth:	Honor your father and mother.
Fifth:	You shall not kill.
Sixth:	You shall not commit adultery.
Seventh:	You shall not steal.
Eighth:	You shall not bear false witness against your neighbor.
Ninth:	You shall not covet your neighbor's spouse.
Tenth:	You shall not covet your neighbor's goods.

PERSONAL ANALYTIC CHART
COMMANDMENTS ~ VICES ~ ADDICTIONS

A COMMANDMENT THAT CHALLENGES ME	
VICES THAT ENSNARE ME	
ADDICTIONS I LIVE WITH	
PERSONS/EVENTS THAT GENERATE FEAR, ANGER OR GRIEF	
PERSONS/EVENTS THAT GENERATE FAITH, HOPE OR LOVE	
STORYLINES IN BOOKS, MOVIES. THAT ALWAYS BRING ME TO TEARS	
WHAT ALWAYS MAKES ME ANGRY	
WHAT ALWAYS MAKES ME GRATEFUL AND MORE SELFLESS	
WHAT ALWAYS MAKES ME FEARFUL AND MORE SELF-CENTERED	

Night Vigil Week 5

THE RICH YOUNG MAN

Artist Unknown

Be open to all thoughts, feelings, and ideas you have coming from the day. Spend some time talking with God about the things you think significant. Stay here as long as you are comfortable. **Be Alone.**

I. Begin this meditation by asking Jesus to be with you. Ask Jesus to give you the graces he feels will be best for you during this time of the retreat and this time of prayer. Specifically, ask for the grace to know the good you desire and how you can be tempted to choose the kinds of things in life that don't bring you peace and happiness. Use the *Triple Colloquy* on the back to ask for these graces.

II. Open your Bible to the tenth chapter of Mark, verses seventeen through thirty-one. Before you read, plan to read it slowly so you can visualize the scenes as they really happened; only place yourself in the crowd. Notice all the details of the people, the smells, the sounds, etc. Keep aware of all the thoughts and feelings you had entering this meditation; only now let yourself be distracted by the events as they unfold before you.

What is the dilemma of this person? Can you sense what he may be feeling as he speaks to Jesus and asks him the questions he does? What is the man really looking for? Why does he leave so sad? Stop the man and ask him what he is thinking and feeling as he leaves Jesus. What does he say?

III. Pay attention to your reaction to the events that have unfolded before you. See the man leave the presence of Jesus. Walk up to Jesus from your place in the crowd. You are present before Jesus so no one else in the crowd can hear you. Speak to Jesus about what you have just seen and heard. What do you say? What does he say?

IV. Ask Jesus what specific type of self-centeredness in your own life would prevent you from being a disciple of his. Ask Jesus about any particular type of self-centeredness in your own life that you think may cause you to walk away sad from him like the person you just witnessed. What do you say? What is Jesus' response? Stop and listen. What are you thinking and feeling?

V. Pray: *Take, Lord, and receive all my liberty, my memory, my understanding, and my entire will; all that I have and possess. You have given all to me. To you, Lord, I return it. Everything is yours; dispose of it according to your will. Give me only your love and your grace. That is enough for me. Amen!*

TRIPLE COLLOQUY OF SAINT IGNATIUS

First Colloquy, or conversation, will be with Mary. Speak with Mary, using your own words asking her to obtain from her Son the grace to follow her Son selflessly in every act and decision of your life. When you finish this conversation, pray the *Hail Mary* slowly, thinking of the words and the person to whom you are praying.

> *Hail Mary, full of grace The Lord is with thee.*
> *Blessed art thou amongst women*
> *and blessed is the fruit of thy womb, Jesus.*
> *Holy Mary, Mother of God, Pray for us sinners,*
> *Now and at the hour of our death.*
> *Amen.*

Second Colloquy, or conversation, will be with Jesus. Speak directly to Jesus, asking him to request his Father for the same graces as above, i.e., that you may follow Jesus. When you finish your conversation, pray the *Anima Christi* slowly, thinking of the words and the person to whom you are praying.

> *Soul of Christ, sanctify me. Body of Christ, save me.*
> *Blood of Christ, fill me. Water from the side of Christ wash me.*
> *Passion of Christ, strengthen me. O Good Jesus, hear me.*
> *Within thy wounds, hide me. Permit me not to be separated from thee.*
> *From the wicked foe, defend me. At the hour of my death, call me,*
> *And bid me come to thee that with thy saints*
> *I may praise thee forever and ever.*
>
> *Amen.*

Third Colloquy, or conversation, will be with God the Father. Ask the Father directly in your own words to give you the graces so you may follow His Son. When you finish, pray the *Our Father,* thinking of the words and the person to whom you are praying.

Our Father, Who art in heaven Hallowed be thy name.
Thy Kingdom come. Thy will be done,
On earth as it is in heaven.
Give us this day our daily bread,
And forgive us our trespasses,
As we forgive those who trespass against us.
Lead us not into temptation,
But deliver us from evil.
Amen.

WEEK 6

DAY ONE

Spiritual Exercise for Day True Heart Time

We continue today with our spiritual exercise exploring connections between different aspects of our history and behaviors to better understand what makes us selfless or self-centered. Fill in the personal spiritual analytic chart below with the goal of writing three things in each category.

As you contemplate the analytic chart, pray for help from the Divine Physician so that you can be completely forthright about *obvious* links between Commandments, vices, addictions and persons or events. Be selfless in confronting self-centeredness! Draw lines linking the connections of what you write down *that are clear to you.*

PERSONAL ANALYTIC CHART
COMMANDMENTS ~ VICES ~ ADDICTIONS
PERSONS ~ EVENTS
DRAW LINES BETWEEN OBVIOUS CONNECTIONS IN THE FOUR CATEGORIES

THREE COMMANDMENTS I AM MOST CHALLENGED IN LIVING	THREE VICES THAT ENSNARE ME	THREE ADDICTIONS I LIVE WITH	THREE PERSONS/EVENTS THAT CAUSE FEAR, ANGER OR GRIEF

DAY TWO

Spiritual Exercise for Day True Heart Time

Contemplate the next personal analytic chart. In it you can see how sin impacted the life of St. Ignatius, especially links in his original (root), core (trunk), and manifest (fruit) sins. You'll also see questions for you to answer in your journal.

VISIBLE SINS

The Fruits & Ornamentation

(Ignatius' addictive gambling, reactive anger, and sexual self-indulgence)

How do you manifest Fear, Anger, moral weaknesses, vices, addictions, and sinful habits that are the most visible to you?

CORE SINS

The Trunk & Superstructure

(Ignatius' arrogance, blinded conscience, and self-centeredness)

How do disobedience and self-centeredness, along with their related fear, anger, and grief,

form the trunk or superstructure of your daily life, feeding on originating sins and events?

↓   ↑

ORIGINAL SINS

The Roots & Foundation

(Original Sin and concupiscence that wounded Ignatius' heart and soul; distinctive family/clan sin and/or early life-events that wounded him spiritually, psychologically and physically)

How do ancient, originating events that rooted the patterns of disobedience and self-centeredness along with its Fear, Anger, Grief manifest in your life?

DAY THREE

Spiritual Exercise for Day True Heart Time

Our short exercise today helps us again to see the difference in our lives between selflessness and self-centeredness. To help with this exercise, feel free to contemplate the elements from the personal analytic charts you filled in earlier. Pray for the grace to see more clearly how sin and self-centeredness have impacted you at the roots, trunk and fruit of your life.

For each of the blank spaces on the next chart, write those elements (at least one each) that you believe are present in your life as:

Original Sins → Root
Core Sins → Trunk
Manifest Sins → Fruit

If you are finding any of this difficult, you can turn not only to prayer for help— prayers that give your voice the ear of the Divine Physician using your personal name for God—but you can also, if you feel it is appropriate, talk about all of this with your companion or mentor.

PERSONAL ANALYTIC CHART
LOOKING FOR LINKS IN MY STORY

MY MANIFEST SINS—THE FRUIT FROM MY TREE

Example: I am constantly envious of other's talents.

↓   ↑

MY CORE SINS—THE TRUNK OF MY TREE

Example: My envy is linked to my desire to always want
to be the best the center of attention.

↓   ↑

MY ORIGINAL SINS—THE ROOTS OF MY TREE

Example: I always felt growing up that my older siblings were praised for their talents and
that I was never paid attention to and this wounded my pride. making me self-centered.

DAY FOUR

Spiritual Exercise for Day True Heart Time
MY WHOLE-LIFE CONFESSION

In the past few weeks, you have been on a treasure hunt, pulling together many diverse elements of your life story. While the long process of piecing your story together will happen throughout the rest of your life-—both by your careful attention and by the grace of God—it entered a new phase of your life in this True Heart program.

And now, this week, everything you have done up to this point will take on greater meaning for you. Because the last week's training exercises bring a great deal of your past together to prepare your Whole-Life Confession. As you move through this week, refer to some of what you wrote in the last weeks and realize the tremendous spiritual effort you have accomplished. You have seen into your core being and are noticing great differences between selflessness and self-centeredness. Now your "seeing" will take a sacramental form in your Whole-Life Confession

A Whole-Life Confession is the opportunity of reconciliation for all the interconnected patterns of selflessness and self-centeredness and of grace, sin and difficulties across *your whole life*. The Confession helps you ask for God's

help to see the big picture of your life—your story—with Christ as your Merciful Divine Physician, forgiver and healer by your side.

As St. John Paul II said in the Catechism:
This reconciliation with God leads to other reconciliations which repair the other breaches caused by sin. The forgiven penitent is reconciled with himself in his inmost being, where he regains his innermost truth. He is reconciled with his brethren whom he has in some way offended and wounded. He is reconciled with the Church. He is reconciled with all creation.[19]

In this way, your Whole Life Confession is a letter to Christ based on your spiritual diagnosis achieved by these weeks of prayerful training. You will now be able to confess current issues and past issues that have been overlooked. As you do this, you are telling Christ the chronic *patterns* of sin and weaknesses that your prayer and reflection, with the help of God's grace, have shown you.

With all this in mind, look at your life story with Christ the Divine Physician beside you. Address Him directly and acknowledge why you need Him as your Savior. This *could* be the very first time you have reviewed your life, seen clearly why you cannot save yourself, and directly asked Jesus to be your Savior. What a profound grace to know you cannot save yourself and to ask Christ for this tremendous gift!

There is no greater gift you give to Christ than your sinfulness and weaknesses as you ask for His healing love, mercy and forgiveness. By doing so, you take seriously the gift of His life, passion, death and resurrection. In this whole process, you will show that you are not afraid to look at your life from Christ's perspective, too. As you tell Jesus you need His cross to be healed you are thanking him for suffering and dying for *you* so that you can be renewed in Him.

---

[19] *Catechism of the Catholic Church* (CCC) 1469--John Paul II, RP 31, 5.

❖

What follows are a few suggestions to help you prepare for this simple, holy and graced letter – this statement of your need and confession of your patterns of sin from a lack of selflessness and an indulgence in self-centeredness, as well as a request for forgiveness, healing and hope.

Read these suggestions today and let them work in your heart as you begin to write notes down or pieces of your Letter to Jesus.

You will have the rest of the week to write the full Letter.

1.   *One thousand words or less—*
Write a letter to Christ that is *no more* than 1000 words. I repeat: write *no more* than 1000 words. It is best to write long-hand so that you are connected heart and mind to your text. If you want a visual of 1000 words, it would be the amount of text from the start of this day's exercise through #4 below. And that is the maximum you are to write!

2.   *Personal words that are heartfelt—*
Early on you identified the name for God that touches your heart. This week find the name for Christ that speaks to your heart. Perhaps it is Christ Jesus, Lord and Savior or My Lord. This week, you will speak directly to Christ Jesus. You are speaking to the One who won your victory and who came into the world to save you.

Speak to Jesus in the first person like this: "Christ Jesus, please forgive my sin of
_____."
"Jesus I remember_____."
"Lord I suffered_____."
"Christ please heal me of my addiction to_____."

"Christ Jesus please heal my anxiety about _____."

Write the confessional story—your history—directly from your heart to the heart of Jesus.

3.   Strive for honesty—

Strive earnestly for courage and honesty in your letter. The letter is for you to read in Whole-Life Confession. You need not impress anyone. Be honest about the forgiveness you need to extend to yourself and to others. *Write from your TRUE HEART.*

4.   You are not climbing Mount Everest—

Pray for the grace not to turn this simple, graced letter/confession opportunity into a huge, exhausting task. You are not climbing a mountain. You are having a conversation with Christ about your life. Hear Him say to you:

Come to me, all you who labor and are burdened, and I will give you rest. Take my yoke upon you and learn from me, for I am meek and humble of heart; and you will find rest for your selves. For my yoke is easy and my burden light. Matthew 11: 28-29

5.   Pray for Patience and Compassion—

Being a True Heart will take the rest of your life. It takes a lifetime for Christ's work of healing and forgiveness to transform your heart and soul. There is no finish line or final enlightenment you can reach on this earth. You will always need healing at deeper levels. You will constantly grow in love, selflessness and humility until the day you pass from this earth. You will not be finished until the day the Divine Physician sits you down at His Eternal Banquet.

But as for the seed that fell on rich soil, they are the ones who, when they have heard the word, embrace it with a generous and good heart, and bear fruit through perseverance. Luke 8:15

Pray to know patience in your journey.

6.   *Set the scene in your heart's imagination—*
If you have any difficulty doing this Letter, imagine that you have been given the opportunity to be alone with Christ when He is walking from one town to another. He says to you: "I will have 15-minutes with you, dear one, just with you alone before I must turn my attention to those others." See the road and the other followers walking up ahead of you but notice that no one else can hear you—just Christ Jesus.

When you start writing your letter (which you will do two days from now) write as if you are speaking to Christ personally He knows why you want to speak with Him and is ready to hear you.

See him look you in the eyes just before you begin talking about your life.

Hear him say, "Soon I will be lifted up on my cross. I will do this for you so that you can find forgiveness, healing and hope for the sins, weaknesses and suffering you experience in your life. As I conquer all death and sin-—as I breathe my last breath—-I will hold you and your life story in my heart. You will find victory and eternal life in me and one day you will be with me in paradise."

Reread these instructions throughout the week if necessary.

Don't write anything yet—just hold all of this in your True Heart today and tonight.

DAY FIVE

Spiritual Exercise for Day True Heart Time
MY LETTER TO CHRIST JESUS

Here is Part One (of three parts) of your actual letter, your confession, to Christ Jesus, the Divine Physician.

Write these two sections of our letter in your Day or Evening True Heart Time today.

✠ "Dear Jesus, I am so grateful for all the gifts you have given to me." (Spend some time writing from your heart why you are grateful. Use Jesus' name often and give *very particular* examples of why you are grateful).

Then move to:

✠ "Lord, I am profoundly aware of how some of my past experiences, life history, family, friends, work, school, neighbors are linked to areas where I find a lack of freedom in my life. These experiences have created embarrassing and/or discouraging habits and rooted patterns of sinfulness." (Now use the other exercises you've completed as a way of looking back over your life. Offer particular examples to Jesus that capture the links and patterns of self-centered sins, addictions, vices, and commandments that cause you to stumble).

If you cannot discern exact patterns yet, simply speak about these areas individually. If there are central people in your life story who are linked to these destructive patterns, mention them to Christ.

If you are confused about some of the things you do, tell Jesus what they are and then ask for His help to better understand why you do what you do.

From your heart, ask Christ's grace to gain greater freedom from these patterns of sin and self-centeredness, habits and vices.

DAY SIX

Spiritual Exercise for Day True Heart Time
MY LETTER TO CHRIST JESUS

Now, as part two (of three parts) of your letter to Christ Jesus write these two sections of your letter in your Day or Evening True Heart Time today.

✠   "Lord, there is one central pattern of sin and self-centeredness that causes me the most embarrassment, shame, confusion and discouragement." (Spend some time being very specific in your conversation with Jesus about this pattern of sin and self-centeredness in your life and why it is so difficult for you. Tell Jesus the particular circumstances in which you seem to fall under the spell of sin the most. Tell Jesus how you feel when you fail. If there are specific incidents of this pattern of failure that you have not confessed, tell them to the Lord, and ask for His healing and forgiveness).

Then move to:

✠   "Lord Jesus, I have come to realize that I cannot save myself and I ask for your compassion. I ask that you be my Savior. Rescue me and be with me all the rest of my days." (Spend some time speaking with Jesus, in very particular words, about why you have come to realize you cannot save yourself and why you need His grace—why you need Him to be your Savior).

Be boldly honest. Tell Him in very clear words why you know—because of x, y and z— you cannot save yourself.

Tell Him about any persons you cannot forgive and what they did to you. Tell Him why it is difficult for you to forgive them. Tell Jesus that with His grace you can desire to forgive them, and in time you will be able to forgive them and ask humbly but clearly for that grace.

Ask the Lord to keep His attention on the core issues in your life (name them) that constantly trip you up. Pray that you never tire in seeking His forgiveness and that you never lose hope in yourself or in Him.

Ask the Lord to be your Savior.

DAY SEVEN

Spiritual Exercise for Day True Heart Time
MY LETTER TO CHRIST JESUS

Now, for the third part of your letter to Christ Jesus, write these two sections in your Day or Evening True Heart Time today.

✠ Lord Jesus, I thank you that you have given me the courage to face any fears I had and to trust you with my life in this healing sacrament of your redeeming love." (As you near the end of your letter and confession, end with very personal words from your heart, thanking Jesus that He has heard your prayer and that He will always be your Savior).

Thank Jesus that He understands your life and ask that He continue to walk with you, give you grace, and be with you till the end of your days. Ask Jesus for the grace to serve Him more each day with everything you think, say and do.

Ask for the grace to work for fruit that will endure to eternity.

Then move to:
✠ End your letter by these words or words just like them, "Thank you, Jesus, for being my Savior." In this ending to your Letter you will be asking for His continued grace as He transforms you into a *TRUE HEART*.

Now you should have your Letter, *your* Confession, in your journal. Hold it close to your heart and set a time in the next week to bring it to the Sacrament of Reconciliation.

Night Vigil Week 6

THE LOST SON AND THE DUTIFUL SON

Le Retour du fils prodigue, Michael Martin Drolling (Wikimedia Commons)

Spend fifteen to forty-five minutes on this meditation. Do only one section at a time and do not read ahead. Do not feel compelled to finish the whole sheet. Stay with each section until your heart suggests moving on. **Be Alone.**

I. Gather in what your senses are experiencing. Breathe in the Spirit of God. Breathe out whatever is troubling, distracting, or burdensome. Be aware of all the thoughts and feelings coming from the day so far.

II. Talk to Jesus in your own words about your desire for this particular grace: that I may come to know lifestyles that give life and those that do not. Ask Jesus for a discerning heart that you may choose the path of life and always turn away from the path of death. Stay with this for as long as you like. Don't feel compelled to move on unless your heart suggests.

III. We read in the story of the lost son and the dutiful son that both the life of self-centeredness and the life of self-righteousness are wrong. Both the son who broke all the Commandments and the one who self-righteously followed them all were both lost. Lifestyles that have the appearance of goodness can be as death-dealing as those that openly violate Gospel values. In Luke chapter fifteen, verses eleven to thirty-two, read the very familiar Gospel story of these two sons and the father who loves them. Visualize their lives as you read the story and see the emptiness and self-centeredness from which they both suffered.

As you watch their lives, see if you have in your own life any of the temptations of the lost or the dutiful son. Listen to their lives and your own. Most especially, feel the embrace of the Father who loves you and will always welcome you home—even when you have strayed from his house and have been lost in self-centeredness.

Then watch the crowd as Jesus tells the story. Who in the crowd do you see living a life of self-indulgence and who a life of legalistic duty? See and experience the events as they happen. Notice everything about what is happening to Jesus and yourself. Do not move to the next section unless your heart suggests.

Pray with Luke 15: 11-32

IV. ASK THE LORD FOR HIS HELP in letting go of the self-centeredness that binds you; of what keeps you from freely coming home if you have strayed, or from accepting the joy of those who have been lost but now are found by the Father's Mercy. Pray that Jesus make you a selfless True Heart.

V. Following the meditation, bring your own prayer period to a close by slowly praying the *Our Father*, listening to the words in your heart as you pray.

WEEK 7

DAY ONE

Spiritual Exercise for Day True Heart Time

Read the following familiar story told in a new way and reflect on the questions.

In the beginning, when God created our human nature, the energy field that is our body and spirit was in complete harmony and we lived before God in complete selflessness. That perfect balance "created" by God is why we were immortal. Our human nature, in this state of original innocence, was completely oriented selflessly toward God.

Because God made us in in the Divine image, we had to be free to accept or reject God's gift of love and immortality. We had to be free to reject selflessness and become self-centered. The pure spiritual beings in the heavens God created were also free to accept or reject God's love—to be selfless or self-centered.

Some of those spiritual beings did reject God and then selfishly sought to destroy God's creation. The main way they could destroy God's creation was to corrupt the beings God made in God's likeness: to turn them from selflessness to self-centeredness. If corrupted, humans would be susceptible to selfishly destroying each other and creation itself.

The greatest tragedy since the beginning of time is that we rejected God's life and surrendered selfless freedom and peace for self-centered constraint and anxiety. At this pivot point, we broke the unified field between spirit and body and we not only lost our innocence but our immortality.

From the point of corruption onwards to right now, spiritual discernment-- including developing radar for selflessness and self-centeredness—is an essential discipline for us. I know you, like me and everyone we know, has felt original sin inside you. You know how easy it is to give in to self-centeredness and how challenging it can be to choose selflessness.

If we are to find our way home to our self-less True Heart, we must learn to master this spirit-body discipline of spiritual discernment.

Reflection Questions:

--What is the first instance I can remember being confronted with a choice between good and evil in the form of selflessness vs. self-centeredness?

--What was the context? What did the struggle feel like?

--What did I choose: selflessness or self-centeredness?

--What were the consequences of my choice?

If you want, write a very short two-sentence reflection in your True Heart Training Log about this experience.

DAY TWO

Spiritual Exercise for Day True Heart Time

Read this for your Day Training Exercise and reflect on the questions below.

Because we have a human nature that can connect with good or evil spiritual energy, we want to learn how it reaches us. Today's training looks at three distinct sources of spiritual energy or "inspirations" that can guide our thoughts, words and deeds.

Saint Ignatius learned about these spiritual energy sources by careful attention to his affective states. That is why True Heart exercises invite you to tune out the electronic world so you can hear the spiritual world. Saint Ignatius learned Inspirations affecting your human nature (spirit-body) originate from three *different* sources:

1. Spiritual energy inspirations can originate from your own life-energy or spirit.

2. Spiritual energy inspirations can originate from a Divine source: the *Divine-Inspirer*.

3.   Spiritual energy inspirations can originate from a demonic source, the *enemy of human nature*: the *counter-inspirer*.

There are three *sources* of spiritual energy inspiration, but only two spiritual energy *states*. St. Ignatius names the two spiritual energy states *consolation* and *desolation*.

The spiritual energy of consolation is when one *experiences*, to a lesser or greater degree, an *increase in faith, hope and love*. The spiritual energy of desolation is when one *experiences*, to a lesser or greater degree, *a loss of faith, hope and love*.

Our Quick Review

Sources of Inspiration

Human nature as an energy source of spirit/body
God as the *Divine-Inspirer*
The enemy of human nature as the *counter-inspirer*

Types of Inspiration

Spiritual Energy of Consolation—increase of faith, hope, love and selflessness
Spiritual energy of Desolation—decrease of faith, hope, love and selflessness

Reflection Questions

Pray to the Divine-Inspirer to have your memory "energized." Use the name for God-the Divine-Inspirer—you discovered in Week 4.

Ask for the grace to remember one time that your radar picked up the spiritual energy of consolation where you experienced an increase of faith, hope, love and selflessness. What was the event/experience and what would you guess was the source? REMEMBER!

Next, pray to the Divine Inspirer to have your memory "energized" again. Ask for the grace to remember one time when your radar picked up the spiritual energy of desolation where you had a decrease in faith, hope, love and selflessness. What was the event/experience and what would you guess was the source? REMEMBER!

Briefly write one or two sentences in your True Heart Training Log about each memory that captures the experience and how you felt during these two different "energized states" and the source from which you think they originated.

For Example: "Today when I invited Greg to come on the weekend camping trip with our group he realized people care about him. Seeing him smile made me feel great and I knew I had done the right thing. His smile made me feel faith, hope and love."

For Example: "When Kimberly asked if she could come with our group to the game, I was not honest and told her we had no more room. Seeing her disappointment made me feel bad about my lack of honesty and what it did to her really decreased my faith, hope love and selflessness."

DAY THREE

Spiritual Exercise for Day True Heart Time
YOU HAVE A RADAR FOR SELFLESS JOY

First Benchmark Strategy for a True Heart's Spiritual Discernment

We can collaborate with spiritual entities that lead us to an immortality of happiness and selflessness or loneliness and self-centeredness. God has given us spiritual radar to help us follow the path to eternal selflessness and reject the path of eternal self-centeredness.

To help your awakening and initiation into the spiritual discernment of a True Heart, two benchmark guidelines will be beneficial in many life situations.

As I lead you in this work I want to speak a truth it has taken me a long time to accept: Divine inspiration, or consolation, does not always *feel good*. It is hard work sometimes. It feels like a struggle sometimes. That is okay.

Equally important is to realize that an unholy inspiration, or spiritual desolation, does not always *feel bad*. Temptation and evil can feel great. That is not okay.

We will explore this seeming paradox in a future reflection.

This first benchmark deals with energy-inspirations that come from the Creator of human nature. These, if followed, ultimately lead to eternal selfless joy.

Benchmark One: Authentic divine energy-inspirations called consolations will have specific features. Consolations will:

1) Increase your True Heart's love for God, family, and others

2) Increase the virtues of humility, self-generosity and selflessness

3) Not oppose the truths and teachings of Scripture, the Tradition and the teaching Church.

God's Direct Action—Consolation can be the consequence of the Divine Physician's Spirit working in you. This form of consolation helps strengthen your heart and soul, encouraging you to turn to God whenever you need spiritual and moral help. Consolation helps you to choose thoughts, words and deeds that express your authentic selfless human nature—your True Heart—made in the Divine image.

God's Action Though Your Human Nature—Consolation can also be the result of your Divinely-shaped human nature expressing itself through your daily life. God created your human nature as a gift in the Divine image and likeness. In spite of Original Sin's impact, cooperating with God's grace activates embedded life forces of your Divinely-shaped human nature. These strengths can help you heal biochemical, physiological and emotional imbalances; energize you; and enable thoughts, words and deeds that express your authentic selfless human nature—your True Heart—made in the Divine image.

Reflection Questions

Pray to the Divine-Inspirer to have your memory "energized." Ask for the grace to remember one time that your love for God and/or other people was stirred in you. What was the context? Remember and briefly write the context and experience below or in your journal.

Example: "I remember on a first-year retreat we had a Mass that made me feel a part of not just my class, but something much bigger. That to me was a time I really felt God and really felt great about the whole world."

Then ask for the grace to remember one time that you were inspired to be more humble, selfless and giving of yourself to others. What was the context? Remember and briefly write the context and experience below or in your journal.

Example: "I remember when I won class president and my main opponent lost. I knew how I would feel if I had lost and I asked her to serve with me as my vice-president."

Ask for the grace to remember one time when you were inspired to follow the teachings of the Scriptures, Catholic Tradition or the Church that stirred your faith, hope and love. What was the context? Remember and briefly write the context and experience below or in your journal.

Example: "I read Tim Tebow's five reasons why not to have sex before marriage and really agreed with him. I decided that I would make it a goal for my life to deepen my faith and pray that I find someone worth spending my life with.

DAY FOUR

Spiritual Exercise for Day True Heart Time

THEME: YOU HAVE A RADAR FOR SELF-CENTERED LONELINESS

Second Benchmark Strategy for a True Heart's Spiritual Discernment

We can collaborate with spiritual entities that lead us to an immortality of happiness and selflessness or loneliness and self-centeredness. God has given us spiritual radar to help us follow the path to eternal selflessness and reject the path of eternal self-centeredness.

This benchmark deals with counter energy-inspirations that come from the enemy of human nature. These, if followed, ultimately lead to eternal self-centered loneliness.

Benchmark Two: Authentic counter-inspirations called desolations will have specific features. Desolations will:

1) Increase self-centeredness, displacing God and others from your True Heart

2) Decrease obedience and humility, and increase pride and self-satisfaction

3)   Arouse hungers and desires that, although they feel good, will typically contradict the truths and teachings proposed by the Scripture, Tradition, and the teaching Church.

The Enemy's Direct Action: The author of counter-inspirations is opposed to Christ and will lead you away from life and truth. Counter-inspirations will produce desires *that feel authentic* because they are linked to *fallen* human nature's physical lusts and spiritual pride. They are the familiar default drives of a broken heart and a sin-damaged human nature.

This form of desolation helps weaken your heart and soul, encouraging you to turn from God. Desolation helps you choose self-centered thoughts, words and deeds that are opposed to your Divinely-shaped human nature—your True Heart.

The Enemy's Action Though Your Sin-Damaged Human Nature: Desolation can also be the consequence of your own sin-damaged human nature. God created your human nature as a gift in the Divine image and likeness. Yet, because of Original Sin's impact, not cooperating with God's grace erodes embedded life forces of your Divinely-shaped human nature, helping to undermine biochemical, physiological, emotional and spiritual balance; de-energizing you; and increasing thoughts, words and deeds that are in opposition to your authentic selfless human nature—your True Heart.

Reflection Questions

Pray to the Divine-Inspirer to have your memory "energized." Ask for the grace to remember one time when your love for God and/or other people was diminished in favor of more self-centered acts or inspirations. What was the context? Remember and briefly write the context and experience below or in your journal.

Example: "I remember on first-year retreat we had a Mass that made me feel left out because I was not chosen as one of the leaders. I was angry about that and did not participate because of it.

Ask for the grace to remember one time that you were inspired to be less humble and giving of yourself to others. What was the context? Remember and briefly write the context and experience below or in your journal.

Example: "I remember when I won class president and my main opponent lost. I knew how I would feel if I lost and I was quietly pleased at her defeat. I could have asked her to serve as my vice-president but intentionally chose someone else instead."

Ask for the grace to remember one time when you were inspired by hungers and desires not follow the teachings of the Scriptures, Catholic Tradition or the Church. What was the context? Remember and briefly write the context and experience in your journal.

Example: "I read Tim Tebow's five reasons why he did not to have sex before marriage and I did not want to be publically ridiculed like him and chose not to follow his advice."

DAY FIVE

Spiritual Exercise for Day True Heart Time
RADAR SIGNALS FROM EITHER THE DIVINE INSPIRER
OR THE COUNTER-INSPIRER
ACT AS HOMING BEACONS FOR YOUR TRUE HEART
TO CAUSE THOUGHTS AND FEELINGS OF
SELFLESS JOY OR SELF-CENTERED LONELINESS

For your True Heart time, read and reflect on this training in discernment. Pay attention to your moods and *feel* the states of consolation and desolation in your True Heart. This process requires a *graced awakening*, so as you read this, please ask God using the name you discovered in Week 4 to give you "eyes to see" your story through the lens of these spiritual lessons. Be patient as you slowly learn this way of understanding your story.

You have learned already that there are three distinct sources influencing your thoughts, words, and deeds.

Both God and the enemy of human nature are aware of your strengths and weaknesses, wounded memories, your SELFLESS JOY and SELF-CENTERED LONELINESS, your hopes, dreams, and fears. God will build on your strengths, inflaming your holy desires, healing what is hurt and broken, and offering ETERNAL FRIENDSHIP to you.

The enemy of human nature seeks to silence your conscience and hide it in shadows. He will work to magnify your problems, diminish your holy desires and inspire a path that leads to hopeless, self-centered loneliness.

You can identify and distinguish Divine inspirations from counter inspirations by their *intellectual* and *affective* traits, or signature characteristics: *consolation and* desolation.

Reflection Questions

Pray to the Divine-Inspirer to have your memory "energized." Ask for the grace to remember one time that you are convinced you received a Divine inspiration that filled you with hope and deepened your love for God and strengthened your commitment to your Catholic faith. Remember. What was the context? Briefly describe the context and experience below or in your journal.

Example: "I remember during a hard time when I went to Sunday Mass and heard the Gospel story of Jesus healing people. I had a dream that night that everything would work out for the best. When I woke up I had chills because I knew God had helped me and I was not afraid anymore and realized how important my faith is to my life."

Pray to the Divine-Inspirer to have your memory "energized." Ask for the grace to remember one time that you are convinced you received a counter-inspiration that seemed right initially, but later diminished your love for God and weakened your commitment to your Catholic faith. Remember. What was the context? Briefly describe the context and experience below or in your journal.

Example: "I remember during a hard time I decided it would be best to miss Sunday Mass so I could go for a run and clear my head. It seemed like the right thing at the time, but later I realized it was a mistake because I did not feel better but more confused. It would have been better to go to Mass and let God help me instead of trying to do it all by myself." I went to confession for missing Mass on Sunday and learned a very valuable spiritual lesson.

DAY SIX

Spiritual Exercise for Day True Heart Time

SPIRITUAL RADAR SIGNALS—WHEN FOLLOWED IN ONE DIRECTION
OR ANOTHER CREATE ENERGY FIELDS OR "LIFESTYLES"
THAT REVEAL WHICH "INSPIRER' YOU ARE FOLLOWING

Remember there really is a Divine-Inspirer who is Lord of the Universe and a counter-inspirer who is the dark lord and the enemy of human nature. These are the real forces that are guiding hearts toward life or death. For this training we focus more sharply on identifying the ways in which these spiritual states manifest in our culture today as lifestyles. Throughout your life today, continue to pay attention to your affective moods to *feel* the states of consolation and desolation in your heart. Look for lifestyle attitudes or choices that bear the signature characteristics of consolation and desolation.

Individuals and groups can consciously or unconsciously live a life that is either aligned with life, selflessness and joy—Gospel Values and a True Heart *or* death, self-centeredness and sadness—a false heart not aligned with the Gospel. The book of Deuteronomy powerfully captures this reality. God placed before the people Israel two distinct choices:

I call heaven and earth today to witness against you: I have set before you life and death, the blessing and the curse. Choose life, then, that you and your descendants may live, by loving the LORD, your God, obeying his voice, and holding fast to him. For that will mean life for you, a long life for you to live on the land which

Remember the key lesson from our previous exercises: things that feel bad can move us towards life and things that feel good can move us towards death.

We have to look not at what makes us feel good or feel bad, but the lifestyles and life-direction feelings move us towards.

the LORD swore to your ancestors, to Abraham, Isaac, and Jacob, to give to them (Dt. 30: 18-20).

If we have become insensitive to God's presence, our True Heart can be moving away from the Author of Life. We may not be aware of this because of a silenced conscience.

If you live in a culture or a sub-culture that is also insensitive to the Author of Life, you can be doubly challenged to find the path back to life—to a True Heart.

When you are sensitive to the Author of life, your *TRUE HEART* is moving in the direction of producing fruit that endures to eternity. This will be correct even if you live in a culture that is insensitive to life's Author.

Christ promises: *Blessed are you when they insult you and persecute you and utter every kind of evil against you [falsely] because of me. Rejoice and be glad, for your reward will be great in heaven. Thus they persecuted the prophets who were before you (Mt 5: 11-12).*

Reflection Question

Pray to the Divine-Inspirer to have your memory "energized." Think of a group you privately supported whose lifestyle was "Gospel-inspired" but it was not popular with the majority of your peers. Perhaps the lifestyle was linked to some hot-button social or moral issue like the environment, sex or marriage, immigration, the economy or politics.

What was the "lifestyle" that made them unpopular? Did you make your support known or keep quiet about it because of fear or majority group pressure?

Write briefly below or in your journal about one of this experience: why did you support the group and how did you act?

DAY SEVEN

Spiritual Exercise for Day True Heart Time
SPIRITUAL RADAR SIGNALS—
LEAD TO LIFESTYLES AND SUBCULTURES

We can choose to align ourselves with sub-cultures that are counter to the life proposed by the Commandments, Scripture and the teaching Church—the life proposed by the very embodiment of human nature, Jesus Christ. It is difficult to be objective about anti-Gospel or "anti-Christ" lifestyles when we are immersed in these sub-cultures or peer groups.

For example, if you get involved with a group of peers that is using or abusing illegal or performance-enhancing drugs, it "sucks you in" and once you are sucked in, it is hard to fully see the damage it is doing to you. That is why we call it a "drug culture." We can embed ourselves in these groups and allow definitions of happiness, success, the good, the beautiful, and the moral to isolate us from the data coming from deep in our divinely inspired True Heart.

These anti-Gospel sub-cultures can be economic, political, artistic, ethnic, intellectual, sexual, athletic, addiction-based, and Web-based or just about anything else that a group endorses. The main challenge is that we can embed ourselves in these cultures, allowing their definitions of happiness, success, the good, the beautiful, and the moral to isolate us from the data coming from deep in our divinely inspired True Heart. Do you see this happening in your friendship groups at school?

So, *consolation* and *desolation* can be ascribed comprehensively as *lifestyles*. By thinking about them that way, we can measure the arc of our lives against the traditional categories of goodness the Church has defined.

Reflection Questions

Pray to the Divine-Inspirer to have your memory "energized." Think of one lifestyle the "majority" defends and one lifestyle the "majority" denounces. Examine each lifestyle in light of whether it aligns or not with the Gospel, Jesus and the Church. Why do you think one is defended and the other denounced?

Example: Pope Francis has denounced gender ideologies saying that there was a war against marriage. He was both praised and ridiculed in the media for this position. He also called for every migrant who needed safety to be allowed in the countries of Europe. He was also praised and ridiculed for this position.

In light of what you have learned about spiritual discernment, write very brief observations below or in your journal about each instance of the rightness or wrongness of what is defended or denounced and what you have come to believe at this point in your True Heart journey.

Reflection Questions

What lifestyles do you engage in that you now realize are *spiritual consolation*?

Are you in lifestyles that you realize now are *spiritual desolation*?

How have you been courageous or fearful in defending what you think is right or wrong with your peers?

Here's how I think I've been courageous…(give an example to your companion)
Here's how I think I've been too scared to speak up…(give an example to your companion).

NIGHT VIGIL WEEK 7

JESUS WALKS ON THE WATER

Jesus Walking on Water by Rebecca Brogran at jtbarts.com

Spend fifteen to forty-five minutes on this exercise. Do only one section at a time and do not read ahead. Do not feel compelled to finish each piece of this. Stay with each section until your heart suggests moving on. Do not read or write after this meditation except perhaps a short journal entry. **Be Alone.**

I. Gather in what your senses are experiencing. Breathe in the Spirit of God. Breathe out whatever is troubling, distracting, or burdensome. Be aware of all the thoughts and feelings coming from the day so far.

II. Talk to Jesus in your own words about your desire for this particular grace: that you may learn to overcome self-centeredness, dread, fear and panic and follow him in selfless faith no matter the storms that rage.

III. Open your Bible and pray with Matthew chapter fourteen, verses twenty-two through thirty-three. Jesus is instructing his disciples that he is the Lord of all Creation and everything is under his command. He is showing his disciples that they must learn to walk in faith by keeping their True Hearts fixed on him and him alone.

Visualize the disciples terrified of Jesus as he walks towards their boat during a raging storm. See the darkness and feel the storm and boat at the point of sinking. See and feel the great fear in the disciples. See also the great love that Peter had for Jesus that leads him to ask Jesus to let him be with him.

Notice: Peter is scared but perseveres but there is still more to learn. When he takes his eyes off of Jesus, he begins to succumb to fear and starts to sink. Notice Jesus rescue him and rebuke him for this lack of faith. Watch and Pray.

IV. ASK THE LORD FOR HIS HELP. Now see yourself with the disciples in the boat. Ask Jesus to let you come to him across the water—to walk by selfless faith. Tell him your fears of walking by selfless faith and ask for the specific help you need to step out of the boat. Mention to him your fears and the patterns you've been remembering in this week's lessons. What does Jesus say to you? What invitation does he extend to you? What help does he give? As you close, say with the other disciples on the boat: "Jesus, you truly are the Son of God!"

V. Following the meditation, bring your own prayer period to a close by slowly praying the *Our Father*, listening to the words in your heart as you pray.

WEEK 8

DAY ONE

Spiritual Exercise for Day True Heart Time
COUNTER-INSPIRATION AS A LIFESTYLE

> *This is an important discernment lesson.* Think of Divine inspiration (spiritual consolation) as a healthy, selfless lifestyle that may not feel healthy because *it is not* supported by the culture or sub-cultures or the peer groups in which you live.
>
> Think of counter inspiration (spiritual desolation) as an unhealthy, self-centered lifestyle that might not feel unhealthy because *it is* supported by the culture or sub-cultures or the peer groups in which you live.
>
> Always *keep an eye on the direction the inspirations lead,* more than whether inspirations make you *feel good* or *feel bad.*

Are you *evolving* under the counter inspirations opposed to true love?

Are your thoughts, words and deeds self-centered and opposed to the Commandments, Scripture and the teaching Church?

The enemy of your human nature is able to hold you in the grip of self-centered false loves by deceit and deceitful appearances. How? What leads you away from God, from Love, appears pleasurable, and is presented as good, morally right, life-giving, fashionable, and enlightened. The false loves are like a drug for the interior pain we feel.

Reflection Exercise:
Pray to the Divine-Inspirer to have your memory "energized."

Map some of the influences in your life using the small chart below of two sub-cultures or peer groups where you spend most of your time each week: school culture, work environments, Internet, social groups and associations, exercise or athletic environments, groups aligned with arts and or entertainment, political parties, and the cultures of film, television and or gaming where you spend time.

Next to the two sub-cultures, write one sentence about what you believe is its *signature characteristic* regarding its *overall* influence on your lifestyle. Does it lead to selflessness or self-centeredness—to God and your faith or away?

If it is self-centered and leads away, write one sentence about how you could leave it or minimize its negative impact on you.

Sub-Culture or Peer Group	Key Characteristics of the Group

Beloved,
do not trust every spirit
but test the spirits
to see whether they belong to God,
because many false prophets
have gone out into the world.

1 Jn 4: 1

DAY TWO

Spiritual Exercise for Day True Heart Time
HOW TO RESPOND WHEN SIGNALS FROM THE DARKNESS
TRICK YOU TO TURN FROM THE LIGHT

Diffusing Counter Inspirations

Ignatius offers four principles for how we ought to act when tempted by the counter inspirations of desolation. Here the first two:

1) *When we are spiritually desolate – experiencing self-centeredness and a loss of faith, hope and love – we should NEVER change course away from the positive resolutions and decisions we reached while previously under the influence of the Divine inspiration of consolation.* **This means: True Hearts must be vigilant when tempted by an urgent or compelling impulse *to act immediately.***

If you are in an emergency situation, of course, you must act quickly, but Ignatius is talking here about the feeling of anxious urgency to reach a decision or engage an action that really needs more patience. For instance, you might know in your heart that you should wait another week to make a decision about something hugely important to you but you just impulsively decide. This may end up being a course change that you regret later.

2) *During times of desolation, redouble efforts to open and orient your heart to God and act selflessly. Use prayer, examination of conscience, and perhaps some simple penance or fasting to seek God's grace (Mk 9:29).*

Reflection Exercise

Pray to the Divine-Inspirer to have your memory "energized." Remember a time when you were on a peaceful good course but then counter-inspirations upset you. The upset compelled you to make a hasty decision and looking back you can see you acted on fear, not peace. What was the context? Remember the anxiety you felt.

Now remember a time when you were upset and turned to prayer and your spiritual disciplines for help and you found peace and calm. What was the context? Remember the relief you felt.

Briefly write these memories below or in your journal.

Counter inspirations make it difficult to *see and feel* authentic human nature—your True Heart. Increasing positive efforts on spiritual fronts might feel incredibly difficult.

Yet St. Ignatius' experience demonstrated that we need at these times *extra exercise* of spirit and body to resist desolation. A determined spirit is necessary during such times.

Also, be attentive to thoughts, words, or deeds that are based on *inaccurate* assessments of your authentic human nature. Allow the times of desolation to instruct you!

DAY THREE

Spiritual Exercise for Day True Heart Time
SPIRITUAL RADAR SIGNALS
HOW GOD SUPPORTS YOU WHEN SIGNALS FROM THE DARKNESS
HAVE TRICKED YOU TO TURN FROM THE LIGHT

Diffusing Counter Inspirations

You have studied Ignatius' first two principles for how we ought to act when tempted by the counter inspirations of desolation and here are the last two:

3) *God provides the essential support and grace necessary to withstand these times of trial and purification.*

The support you need will come from your natural abilities, assisted by Divine grace. You may feel completely overwhelmed by temptations or the darkness of spirit associated with disordered attractions and compulsive behaviors. Yet there is sufficient grace for salvation, even if the *logic* of the counter inspiration indicates otherwise! Jesus, the Divine Physician, is *very close to you* during these times of purification. Through trial and error, St. Ignatius learned that God is *not* absent.

When you do not feel the Spirit, consciously *thank God, who in complete faithfulness,* will embrace you. Thank God *aloud* and affirm God's salvific role in your *TRUE HEART*.

4) Intentionally strive to cultivate patience and persevere in the religious practices of your faith when influenced by the desolation of counter-inspiration.

FOOTPRINTS IN THE SAND

One night I dreamed I was walking along the beach with the Lord. Many scenes from my life flashed across the sky.

In each scene I noticed footprints in the sand. Sometimes there were two sets of footprints, other times there was one only.

This bothered me because I noticed that during the low periods of my life, when I was suffering from anguish, sorrow or defeat, I could see only one set of footprints, so I said to the Lord,

"You promised me Lord, that if I followed you, you would walk with me always. But I have noticed that during the most trying periods of my life there has only been one set of footprints in the sand. Why, when I needed you most, have you not been there for me?"

The Lord replied, "The years when you have seen only one set of footprints, my child, is when I carried you."

Mary Stevenson, 1936

The Divine inspiration of consolation always returns but in the interim, we must use the divine means of prayer, penance, and self-examination and acts of selflessness to resist and gain the most from these times of trial. In this way, we can embrace desolation as an opportunity to deepen our maturing life with God. Do Not Be Afraid.

Reflection Exercise:

Pray to the Divine-Inspirer to have your memory "energized." Remember!

What is the one experience or event that makes you question God's love for you? Say it aloud. Now hear the Lord say: "Nothing in the past or the future; no angel or demon; no height or depth; nothing in all of creation will ever separate you from my love in Christ Jesus." (Rom 8:38-39).

Write your experience and God's response in your journal.

Example: For me, the most powerful modern poem that captures this faithfulness of God is the Footprints Poem. You know it: It has the same wisdom Ignatius uses about trusting God during difficult times. God never leaves us!

DAY FOUR

Spiritual Exercise for Day True Heart Time
THE FIRST ATTACK STRATEGY OF THE COUNTER-INSPIRER
FEAR AND PANIC ATTACKS

When you engage your faith practice daily, the enemy of human nature can employ three subtle and malicious lines of attack to discourage you. He will use the weaknesses and fears associated with your vices, your sinful appetites, your compulsive behaviors, your spiritual/psychological wounds, and your broken heart.

This week we will consider the first of the three strategies:

1) *Fear and panic attacks are strategically employed to block growth.*

If you stay committed to the process of uprooting vices, sins, addictions and destructive habits from your life, you will often be attacked with waves of fear and panic. These may try to turn your attention away from the True Heart process.

Reflection Question:
Pray to the Divine-Inspirer to have your memory "energized." Remember! Think on the times when you were paralyzed by fear or panic attacks. They would be times too of self-centeredness. What were the "hooks" that triggered

the terrible fear and how did self-centered behaviors manifest themselves? For example: was the "hook" your own perfectionism? Did you have a music recital or a huge game or a big test that you prepared for quite well but as the time of performance got close, you started imagining everything that could go wrong, and before you knew it you felt paralyzed?

Remember an example like this in your experience and then look at it carefully—discern what "triggered" the panic? Did you, for instance, hear someone say something relatively harmless that you "heard" as a scary possibility? "You'll do great, just remember to focus before you act." This comment was innocuous but before you knew it your brain was seeing only all the bad possibilities?

Find your own memories of this kind of paralysis. Sit with the memories for a while. Let yourself understand the deep truth of the attack strategy. It happens to keep you off balance and away from your True Heart. Pray to "see" the wound or previous fears that initiated this pattern in your life.

Briefly write your memory and what you've learned below or in your journal.

Day Five

THE SECOND ATTACK STRATEGY OF THE COUNTER-INSPIRER:
<u>FALSE LOVES DISGUISED AS TRUE LOVES</u>

Consider the second of the three attack strategies used by our Enemy:

2) Self-Centeredness and false values masquerade as true love and authentic values.

The enemy can invade our thinking process to portray narcissism as authentic love and to make us see vices as positive values. "Drinking a lot is fine," we think, "in fact, it's great because it's a way I bond with my friends." Or:
"I am better at _____ than just about everyone else—I'm the best—I've got it made."

Your heart can be easily fooled by false loves. All false loves—of drinking or pride or any other vice – are *lusts* masquerading as *love*. They are mirages for parched and anxious hearts hoping to quench their thirst. Instead of providing lasting peace, these illicit loves and illusions merely intensify self-centeredness, longings, and self-deception.

In all this, there is a seemingly infinite variety of deception and seductions. They are limited only by the numerous ways a heart can be broken. God will not sanction these lusts because they issue from a violated heart and lead to your heart's further violation. Once you act upon a false love or deceptive lust, you will most assuredly violate the hearts of others.

Remember: God is Love: the origin, the end, and the defender of the selfless human heart. While God is infinitely merciful with our struggles, God does not sanction anything that breaks your heart – destroys your own or another person's authentic human nature – or leads to your spiritual death. By not sanctioning false loves in you, God is actually doing you a great favor—protecting you! He does this by not enabling you—and hoping that you will one day, very soon, see through the self-centered deceptions and return fully to his Heart.

Reflection Exercise:
Pray to the Divine-Inspirer to have your memory "energized." Remember! Name your sins, addictions, and bad habits truthfully as self-centered, false lovers. In the light of grace, let one or more of them be revealed as neither true servants of the heart nor pathways to the Divine. Expose them! Focus on the main "false love" you need to see *most clearly right now*. Identify it and do the exercise below. When you are done, write a brief journal entry about what you learned today in this training.

DAY SIX

Spiritual Exercise for Day True Heart Time
THE THIRD ATTACK STRATEGY OF THE COUNTER-INSPIRER
USE A HARDENED HEART TO DEFEND A BROKEN HEART

This week we examine the third attack strategy used by the Enemy to obstruct our spiritual progress. Just as in the first two lines of attack, *fear* is the weapon used against you.

3) *When you commit to uprooting sin, addictions, and vices from your body and soul, you will be assaulted by attacks directed at the spiritual and psychological wounds that make you most vulnerable.*

The enemy of human nature can viciously attack you where past pain and wounds have left you most vulnerable. A wall, built with emotional and intellectual counter-inspirations, is erected around the injuries, darkening your conscience. The enemy's purpose in hardening your heart is to keep your emotional and intellectual defenses firmly in place; to keep your conscience dark and your true human nature *hidden*.

Perhaps you felt very hurt after your parents divorced or after your best friend moved away or being betrayed in a relationship or losing a job to someone else or... In response to the pain you became more hardened in your judgments about the meaning of life, truth and beauty. Many normal things in life soon looked grim to you. You gradually stopped trusting people who love you. You started overreacting to people's ordinary, even loving intentions.

The enemy of human nature's chief goal is to *permanently camouflage* your heart. He loves it when you are wounded—this allows him to build walls in you. Jesus made reference to these forms of defensive structures. He said they keep people from believing in Him, even if He should rise from the dead (Lk 16:31), and they grieved Jesus because they harden hearts (Mk 3: 5).

Reflection Exercise:
Pray to the Divine-Inspirer to have your memory "energized." Remember! Think of one hard-hearted position you have taken that goes against the Gospel's and the Church's teachings of love. Remember all the intellectual arguments you make, internally or with others, that "justify" a position you know in your heart to be too extreme.

Bring your thoughts to Jesus in this exercise. See him sitting with you. Tell him what you believe and why you think yourself justified in holding it. What does Jesus, who is the truth and the model of human nature, say? What does he invite you to understand? Does he challenge you in any way? What do you say in return?

Write your experiences briefly in your journal.
Example: A college senior shared on a retreat how he had lost his virginity in high school. He was deeply in love with the girl and the event took place in his family home. He felt afterward that he betrayed his parent's trust (they were away). And very next day, the girl dumped him. She had simply "used" him for her own pleasure.

Since this was his first sexual relationship, his self-confidence suffered terribly. His heart was hardened twice—once over the shame of having betrayed his parent's trust and once over being "used." Both his relationship with his parents and women suffered. He shut his parents out of his life and started to "use" girls the way he had been used. But he felt justified because of the "hardness of his heart."

He only later realized how his heart had been broken by his own shame and by the pain of being used. It took six years to see how he was treating his parents and women and finally had the grace to change—to "see" what had happened.

DAY SEVEN

Spiritual Exercise for Day True Heart Time
Do You Need To Meet with A Mentor Today?

This meeting does not have to be overscheduled but I hope you will speak with your mentor about the conclusions you reached in your memories and insights regarding the eight strategies in these last two weeks. Ask your mentor to share insights with you on how he has also come to understand the strategies in his life story.

To help you have this conversation, you could "teach" your mentor the eight strategies. You could also pick out one or two that moved you deeply as we studied them together in this journey.

Take a few minutes to reflect on each of the unfinished statements below.

In this conversation, you could say things like this:

"Just like St. Ignatius' Divine inspiration to reform his life was corrupted into a damaging habit of confessing old sins, I've realized that my divine inspiration is corrupted by

_____."

"I know now that the counter-inspirer hurts me by manipulating my long-standing vulnerabilities which are:

_____."

"I understand that the Divine-Inspirer will always offer the graces and insights to lead me home. Here's how I've come to understand this:

_____."

Talk with your mentor about the victory that is assured for you in Christ's birth, life, death and resurrection. Ask your mentor how he learned to fully activate this sense of assurance in his life.

As you work with God's grace to let your life be transformed into *TRUE HEART*, never be discouraged by your failings, sins and weaknesses. The Divine Physician will never tire of forgiving you. Never tire of coming to Him for forgiveness. In this radical, loving trust, you encounter the unfathomable and unbounded mercy of God.

Reflection Exercise:
After talking with your mentor, pray to the Divine-Inspirer to have your memory "energized." Remember!

Write briefly below or in your journal as best as you can recall the one major lesson you learned from the previous eight strategies discussed in the last two weeks of True Heart.

Write a crucial insight you gained from meeting with your mentor.

Pray to be inspired and write briefly in your journal one or two lessons you "never want to forget!" Be brief but specific.

Night Vigil Week 8

THE BEHEADING OF ST. JOHN THE BAPTIST

The Beheading of St. John the Baptist by Pierre Puvis de Chavannes

Spend fifteen to forty-five minutes on this training. Do only one section at a time and do not read ahead. Do not feel compelled to finish the whole exercise. Stay with each section until your heart suggests moving on. Do not read or write after this meditation except perhaps a short journal entry. **Be Alone.**

I. Gather in what your senses are experiencing. Breathe in the Spirit of God. Breathe out whatever is troubling, distracting, or burdensome. Be aware of all the thoughts and feelings coming from the day and week so far.

II. Talk to Jesus in your own words about your desire for this particular grace: that I may learn to love him so much that I would, if the time came, selflessly offer my very life for him and his Leadership in the world. Pray for the grace to be more in love with Christ and his light, than to fear those who follow the enemy in darkness. Pray for the grace to give your life's blood for Christ the King. Stay with this for as long as you like. Don't feel compelled to move on unless your heart suggests.

III. Open your Bible and pray with Matthew chapter fourteen, verses one through twelve. As you read, be aware of this: John the Baptist was the greatest prophet in Israel's history. He is the pivot point between the old and new Covenants. He, like you, was known by Christ in his mother's womb. From the moment Mary visited Elizabeth and the child John leapt, he was blessed by Christ to be the herald of the Lamb of God coming into the world. Like Jesus said, "of those born of women, none is greater than John."

Now see John imprisoned for challenging Herod's marriage. See the party as it unfolds and the hatred and jealously of Herodias' mother. See this courageous prophet in the fullness of his manhood through the pledge of a coward who succumbs to the hatred of his wife. Be at the party. Watch events as they unfold. See, smell, sense all that is happening. Feel Jesus' Spirit from afar sensing what is happening to his herald and champion.

What is in Jesus' heart as he feels John's life ended? Watch and pray. See and experience the events as they happen. Notice everything about what is happening to Jesus and yourself. Do not move to the next section unless your heart suggests.

IV. ASK THE LORD FOR HIS HELP. You are with Jesus as the news is brought to him of John's murder. Hear Jesus say to you: "The least in the Kingdom is greater than John. Do you still want to be my follower knowing the price? What do you say to Jesus? What then, does he say to you in return? Listen.

V. Following the meditation, bring your own prayer period to a close by slowly praying the *Our Father,* listening to the words in your heart as you pray.

WEEK 9

DAY ONE

Spiritual Exercise for Day True Heart Time
LISTENING TO MY STORY

For this week, you will be reviewing the patterns in your life of self-centeredness. This is a holy exercise in spiritual growth that matches St. Ignatius' first week of his Spiritual Exercises. In the First Week, the one making a retreat seeks to understand the elements in his or her life that block the light of the Holy Spirit and render them less than free to follow the inspirations of God in their life.

To understand what takes away your spiritual freedom is to uncover your True Heart. Approach these exercises with great interest as you discover your life story in a wholly new way.

Reflection Exercise:

For today, review your Journal Entries for weeks 1-8 from your True Heart Exercise Logs. In those Journal Entries, you were seeking to understand two trends in your day. For this exercise we are interested in those vain and self-centered actions that decreased your faith, hope and love of God and neighbor.

Review your entries and briefly note below the most significant patterns that come to light that help you understand better the temptations you face to turn inward in a self-centered way.

DAY TWO

Spiritual Exercise for Day True Heart Time
LISTENING TO MY STORY

For this week, you will be reviewing the patterns in your life of vain, self-centeredness. This is a holy exercise in spiritual growth that matches St. Ignatius' first week of his Spiritual Exercises. In the First Week, the one making a retreat seeks to understand the elements in his or her life that block the light of the Holy Spirit and render them less than free to follow the inspirations of God in their life.

To understand what takes away your spiritual freedom is to uncover your True Heart. Approach these exercises with great interest as you discover your life story in a wholly new way.

Reflection Exercise:
For today, review exercises from Weeks 1-4. Specifically, review the following exercises to mine the gold in them that uncovers patterns of self-centeredness in your life story.

Week One-Day Six: Review your entries for this day. Write down any patterns of self-centeredness in your life that you deem major temptations that you want to resist?

Week Two and Week Three: Briefly review your notes from the passages from Mark's Gospel. Write down any patterns of self-centeredness did you discover in your story in light of these Gospel passages that you consider significant temptations that you want to resist in your life?

Week Four: Briefly review your notes on the Ten Commandments. Write down any patterns of self-centeredness that you consider significant temptations that you want to resist in your life.

DAY THREE

Spiritual Exercise for Day True Heart Time
LISTENING TO MY STORY

For this week, you will be reviewing the patterns in your life of vain, self-centeredness. This is a holy exercise in spiritual growth that matches St. Ignatius' first week of his Spiritual Exercises. In the First Week, the one making a retreat seeks to understand the elements in his or her life that block the light of the Holy Spirit and render them less than free to follow the inspirations of God in their life.

To understand what takes away your spiritual freedom is to uncover your True Heart. Approach these exercises with great interest as you discover your life story in a wholly new way.

Reflection Exercise:
Week Five-Day Seven: Briefly review the links between the vices and addictions you discovered and the Ten Commandments. Write down the main patterns of self-centeredness you consider significant that you would like to avoid in your life.

Week Six-Day Four to Seven: Briefly review your Whole-Life Confession. Write down the main pattern of self-centeredness that you want to confess that you consider significant and would like to avoid in your life.

Week Seven and Eight: Briefly review your notes for the exercises on Spiritual Discernment. Write down the three top patterns of self-centeredness that you consider significant that you want to avoid in your life.

DAY FOUR

Spiritual Exercise for Day True Heart Time
WRITING MY STORY

Reflection Exercise:

Today, you are writing part one of a short autobiography of your life. You are looking to the future and imagining you have lived most of your life. You are writing a "future story" as if you had fully given yourself over to a life of self-centeredness. You are to write between two hundred and fifty to three hundred words; about one page of a double-spaced typed page of part one of your autobiography.

The themes you are covering in part one of your self-centered autobiography will deal with your education, your career(s), your wealth and your financial investments. Be very creative, bold and descriptive. Remember; you are writing as if you gave yourself over completely to a self-centered life.

DAY FIVE

Spiritual Exercise for Day True Heart Time
WRITING MY STORY

Reflection Exercise:

Today, you are writing part two of a short autobiography of your life. You are looking to the future and imagining you have lived most of your life. You are writing a "future story" as if you had fully given yourself over to a life of self-centeredness. You are to write between two hundred and fifty to three hundred words; about one page of a double-spaced typed page for part two of your autobiography.

The themes you are covering in part two of your self-centered autobiography will deal with your status as married or single (if married, how many marriages?), your children if you had any, your friends and social circles and a description of your charitable giving. Be very creative, bold and descriptive. Remember; you are writing as if you gave yourself over completely to a self-centered life.

DAY SIX

Spiritual Exercise for Day True Heart Time
WRITING MY STORY

Reflection Exercise:

Today, you are writing part three of a short autobiography of your life. You are looking to the future and imagining you have lived most of your life. You are writing a "future story" as if you had fully given yourself over to a life of self-centeredness. You are to write between two hundred and fifty to three hundred words; about one page of a double-spaced typed page for part three of your autobiography.

The themes you are covering in part two of your self-centered autobiography will deal with your faith practice, your political views/causes if any, the most notable events in your life, any awards you received and that for which you are most notorious. Be very creative, bold and descriptive. Remember; you are writing as if you gave yourself over completely to a self-centered life.

DAY SEVEN

Spiritual Exercise for Day True Heart Time
FAITH PRACTICES TO AVOID A SELF-CENTERED LIFE

Reflection Exercise:

Briefly review all three parts of your self-centered autobiography. Write down the four main spiritual habits and/or practices you would have to incorporate into your regular regimen in order for you not to give yourself over to a life of self-centeredness. Be brief but also say why these particular practices are important as spiritual preventative medicine to self-centeredness.

Night Vigil Week 9

THE PHARISEE AND THE TAX COLLECTOR

The Parable of the Pharisee and the Tax Collector by Rebecca Brogran jbtarts.com

Spend forty-five minutes on this training... Do only one section at a time and do not read ahead. Do not feel compelled to finish the whole vigil quickly. Stay with each section until your heart suggests moving on. Do not read or write after this meditation except perhaps a short journal entry. **Be Alone.**

I. Gather in what your senses are experiencing. Breathe in the Spirit of God. Breathe out whatever is troubling, distracting, or burdensome. Be aware of all the thoughts and feelings coming from the day so far.

II. Talk to Jesus in your own words about your desire for this particular grace: that I may come to know that a True Heart is always humble and never proud in a self-centered way.

Pray to Jesus in very personal words that he gives you the knowledge you are loved, even in your sinfulness and weakness. Pray for the grace to know that Jesus our TRUE HEART, learned obedience by suffering on and the path of humility. Stay with this for as long as you like. Don't feel compelled to move on unless your heart suggests.

III. Open your Bible and pray with Luke chapter eighteen, verses nine to fourteen. Jesus is instructing his disciples whom he wants to be True Hearts and leaders. He must show them that a true leader is always humble and never proud. Visualize the disciples listening to Jesus and the imaginary scene in the temple describes. Does Jesus make the story serious or humorous? How is he trying to get his disciples to see what real leadership is about in how he describes the story. See and experience the events as they happen. Notice everything about what is happening to Jesus and yourself. Do not move to the next section unless your heart suggests.

IV. ASK THE LORD FOR HIS HELP. Imagine that you are with the disciples as Jesus relates the story of the Pharisee and the tax collector. Now imagine that Jesus turns to you in the crowd and repeats the very last line of the story: "Everyone who exalts himself will be humbled, but the person who humbles oneself will be exalted."

How does Jesus say this to you? Does he challenge you or is he praising you? What do you feel as you hear Jesus speak this truth to you? Stop, listen and understand. When you are done, turn to Jesus and say: "Please, Lord, make me a selfless, True Heart."

V. Following the meditation, bring your own prayer period to a close by slowly praying the Our Father, listening to the words in your heart as you pray.

WEEK 10

DAY ONE

Spiritual Exercise for Day True Heart Time
LISTENING TO MY STORY

This week is a mirror exercise from Week 9. You will be reviewing the patterns of selflessness in your life. Like last week, this is a holy exercise in spiritual growth that matches St. Ignatius' conversion and life-transformation detailed in his autobiography and his Spiritual Exercises. In the Fourth Week, the one making a retreat seeks to understand how God labors in all things for our good. You are looking at your life in light of this graced awareness and seeking to see into the future the ideal of selflessness you most want your own life to achieve.

To understand your deepest desires for selflessness is to uncover your True Heart. Approach these exercises like last week's, with great interest. We become what we desire most!

Reflection Exercise:
For today, review your Journal Entries for weeks 1-8 from your True Heart Exercise Logs. In those Journal Entries, you were seeking to understand two trends in your day. For this exercise, we are interested in those selfless actions that increased your faith, hope and love of God and neighbor.

Review your entries and briefly note below the most significant patterns that come to light that help you understand better the deepest desires you long for that move your heart toward selflessness.

DAY TWO

Spiritual Exercise for Day True Heart Time
LISTENING TO MY STORY

This week is a mirror exercise from Week 9. You will be reviewing the patterns of selflessness in your life. Like last week, this is a holy exercise in spiritual growth that matches St. Ignatius' conversion and life-transformation detailed in his autobiography and his Spiritual Exercises. In the Fourth Week, the one making a retreat seeks to understand how God labors in all things for our good. You are looking at your life in light of this graced awareness and seeking to see into the future the ideal of selflessness you most want your own life to achieve.

To understand your deepest desires for selflessness is to uncover your True Heart. Approach these exercises like last week's, with great interest. We become what we desire most!

Reflection Exercise:

For today, review exercises from Weeks 1-4. Specifically, review the following exercises to mine the gold in them that uncovers your deepest desires for selflessness in your life story.

Week One-Day Six: Review your entries for this day. Write down any patterns of selflessness in your life that express your deepest hopes for selfless and who you hope to become.

Week Two and Week Three: Briefly review your notes from the passages from Mark's Gospel. Write down any patterns of selflessness you discover in your story in light of these Gospel passages that you consider significant holy desires of selflessness you want your life to imitate.

Week Four: Briefly review your notes on the Ten Commandments. Write down any patterns of selflessness that you most want your life to imitate.

DAY THREE

Spiritual Exercise for Day True Heart Time
LISTENING TO MY STORY

This week is a mirror exercise from Week 9. You will be reviewing the patterns of selflessness in your life. Like last week, this is a holy exercise in spiritual growth that matches St. Ignatius' conversion and life-transformation detailed in his autobiography and his Spiritual Exercises. In the Fourth Week, the one making a retreat seeks to understand how God labors in all things for our good. You are looking at your life in light of this graced awareness and seeking to see into the future the ideal of selflessness you most want your own life to achieve.

To understand your deepest desires for selflessness is to uncover your True Heart. Approach these exercises like last week's, with great interest. We become what we desire most!

Reflection Exercise:
Week Five-Day Seven: Briefly review the links between the vices and addictions you discovered and the Ten Commandments. Write down the main patterns in light of this exercise that you want to avoid in order to live a selfless life.

Week Six-Day Four to Seven: Briefly review your Whole-Life Confession. Write down the main pattern of holy selflessness that you desire most that is the opposite of what your main temptation(s) to self-centeredness reveals.

Week Seven and Eight: Briefly review your notes for the exercises on Spiritual Discernment. Write down the three top patterns of selflessness that you consider significant that you want to imitate in your life.

DAY FOUR

Spiritual Exercise for Day True Heart Time
WRITING MY STORY

Reflection Exercise:

Today, you are writing part one of a short autobiography of your life. You are looking to the future and imagining you have lived most of your life. You are writing a "future story" as if you had fully given yourself over to a life of selflessness. You are to write between two hundred and fifty to three hundred words; about one page of a double-spaced typed page of part one of your autobiography.

The themes you are covering in part one of your selfless autobiography will deal with your education, your career(s), your wealth and your financial investments. Be very creative, bold and descriptive. Remember; you are writing as if you gave yourself over completely to a selfless life.

DAY FIVE

Spiritual Exercise for Day True Heart Time
WRITING MY STORY

Reflection Exercise:

Today, you are writing part one of a short autobiography of your life. You are looking to the future and imagining you have lived most of your life. You are writing a "future story" as if you had fully given yourself over to a life of selflessness. You are to write between two hundred and fifty to three hundred words; about one page of a double-spaced typed page of part one of your autobiography.

The themes you are covering in part two of your selfless autobiography will deal with your status as married or single (if married, how many marriages?), your children if you had any, your friends and social circles and a description of your charitable giving. Be very creative, bold and descriptive. Remember; you are writing as if you gave yourself over completely to a selfless life.

DAY SIX

Spiritual Exercise for Day True Heart Time
WRITING MY STORY

Reflection Exercise:

Today, you are writing part one of a short autobiography of your life. You are looking to the future and imagining you have lived most of your life. You are writing a "future story" as if you had fully given yourself over to a life of selflessness. You are to write between two hundred and fifty to three hundred words; about one page of a double-spaced typed page of part one of your autobiography.

The themes you are covering in part two of your selfless autobiography will deal with your faith practice, your political views/causes if any, the most notable events in your life, any awards you received and that for which you are most famous. Be very creative, bold and descriptive. Remember; you are writing as if you gave yourself over completely to a selfless life.

DAY SEVEN

Spiritual Exercise for Day True Heart Time
FAITH PRACTICES TO PROMOTE A SELFLESS LIFE

Reflection Exercise:

Briefly review all three parts of your selfless autobiography. Write down the four main spiritual habits and/or practices you would have to incorporate into your regular regimen in order for you to give yourself over to a life of selflessness. Be brief but also say why these particular practices are important as spiritual paths to selflessness.

Night Vigil Week 10

THE BAPTISM OF JESUS

The Baptism of Christ by Tintoretto

Spend forty-five minutes on this training. Do only one section at a time and do not read ahead. Do not feel compelled to finish the whole vigil in each intricate part. Stay with each section until your heart suggests moving on. Do not read or write after this meditation except perhaps a short journal entry. **Be Alone.**

I. Gather in what your senses are experiencing. Breathe in the Spirit of God. Breathe out whatever is troubling, distracting, or burdensome. Be aware of all the thoughts and feelings coming from the day so far.

II. Talk to Jesus in your own words about your desire for this particular grace: that I may always submit to my True Heart and live in humility so I can be one with Jesus and also his disciple – beloved of the Father. May I not be afraid to follow the vocation/mission of selflessness I know in my True Heart for which I have been baptized. May I know in my True Heart that Jesus wants me as his disciple so he can honor me one day in his Kingdom before the Father. Stay with this for as long as you like. Don't feel compelled to move on unless your heart suggests.

III. Open your Bible and pray with John chapter one, verses twenty-four through thirty-four and Matthew chapter three, verses twenty-one and twenty-two. Watch John and Jesus as the events you read unfold. See the crowd. What is their mood? Are they young and old? Be in the crowd watching this pivotal moment in the life of Jesus. See Jesus in the river and watch him as the water is poured over his head and body and notice the expression on his face and on the face of John who baptizes him. Can you sense what Jesus is thinking and feeling? What John is thinking and feeling? What the assembled crowd is thinking and feeling?

IV. ASK THE LORD FOR HIS HELP. After the descent of the Holy Spirit, notice that Jesus sees you in the crowd and invites you to be with him in the Jordan. He reaches out to take your hand. He tells you are beloved to him and he wants you as his disciple. He wants you to live selflessly like himself.

Imagine it just like this. See Jesus take the seashell from John and with water from the Jordan, pour it over your head and body. See how he looks to heaven and tells his Father: "Father (put your name here) is to be with me in my mission. Confirm (put your name here) in the vocation you have placed in (put your name here) True Heart."

How do you feel now? What is the exact vocation/mission of selflessness he has placed on your True Heart? Listen to Jesus' words as he defines your vocation with you—your way of following him into service for others. Let him take both your hands and speak to you from his heart to yours. As he does, feel your common vocation with Jesus: to selflessly bring the Father's light and salvation to the world.

V. Following the meditation, bring your own prayer period to a close by slowly praying the Our Father, listening to the words in your heart as you pray.

TRUE HEART
ALL-NIGHT VIGIL

PREPARATION OF THE PLACE

The TRUE HEART All-Night Vigil is an opportunity for you to conclude the TRUE HEART program and gather the graces for the ten-week journey.[20] You also seek to offer your life to the work of the Kingdom of Christ. It is common in the history of Christianity for an individual to do a "night vigil" when beginning an important mission. Entry into knighthood in medieval times began with an all-night vigil in the chapel of a castle or a major church.

---

[20] Perhaps you might consider it an is a spiritual form of an Outward Bound solo adventure. On the organization's website, there is a quote from the American author, Caroline Myss: "*Always go with the choice that scares you the most, because that's the one that is going to require the most from you.*"

St Ignatius understood this holy ritual. After his conversion, seeking to imitate Christ, he stripped himself of his worldly ways by giving his fine clothes to a poor man. Later, in an all-night vigil before the Black Madonna in the church of the Benedictine abbey at Montserrat, he hung up his sword and dagger. Effectively, his old life was over and his new life desiring only the armor of Christ, had begun.

Black Madonna of Montserrat

You are asking for the graces to dedicate your life to Christ. You may discover the specific way to accomplish this goal during the night vigil. However, the general consecration of your life to the Way, Truth and the Light of Christ is your main spiritual exercise for the evening vigil. Choose this vigil—embrace its profound mysteries and be not afraid!

The time frame mirrors an eight-hour workday, only think of it as night work—spiritual work. Find a Catholic Church that has a 24-hour Adoration Chapel. Find the one as close to your home as possible. Plan to be there from 9,10 or 11 PM in the evening till 5, 6 or 7 AM the following morning. Choose the best eight-hour structure to accommodate your time at the locations that might be available to you.

Contact the parish and let them know who you are and that you would like to do an all-night vigil. Plan the night by including your family in the details of the vigil. Plan not to bring a cell phone. The goal is to be alone with Christ. Embrace the silence and enter the mystery! Christ is truly present to you in the Blessed Sacrament.

Pedro Arrupe in 1909

The first six hours of the vigil will be reflecting on some powerful memories of Fr. Pedro Arrupe, S.J. Fr. Arrupe was the head Jesuit when I entered the order in 1973. His cause for sainthood was begun in the late winter of 2019. I read this article when I was in my mid-twenties and it had a deep impact on me. As you begin your TRUE HEART Night Vigil, I ask you to enter into the mystery of Christ present to you in the Blessed Sacrament. Believing he is real and present and that he loves you, will be the most important work you can accomplish in this life— for this vigil.

I offer this reflection of Fr. Arrupe to help you realize the authentic supernatural power of God that marks Christ's imprint on the world since the time he lived, died and rose again—forever changing your life and the history of the cosmos. Embrace the silence and enter the mystery of life, of Christ and your story.

Below is a small section of what the Church believes about Christ and the Eucharist and His redemptive work. This is the great wonder and mystery that you will be present to during this vigil.

In his desire that all people should be saved and come to the knowledge of the truth, God spoke in former times to our forefathers through the prophets, on many occasions and in different ways. Then, in the fullness of time he sent his Son, the Word made man, anointed by the Holy Spirit, to bring good news to the poor, to heal the broken-hearted as the physician of body and spirit and the mediator between God and men. In the unity of the person of the Word, his human nature was the instrument of our salvation. Thus in Christ there has come to be the perfect atonement that reconciles us with God, and we have been given the power to offer the fullness of divine worship.

This work of man's redemption and God's perfect glory was foreshadowed by God's mighty deeds among the people of the Old Covenant. It was brought to fulfillment by Christ the Lord, especially through the paschal mystery of his blessed passion, resurrection from the dead and ascension in glory: by dying he destroyed our death, and by rising again he restored our life. From his side, as he lay asleep on the cross, was born that wonderful sacrament which is the Church in its entirety.

As Christ was sent by the Father, so in his turn he sent the apostles, filled with the Holy Spirit. They were sent to preach the Gospel to every creature, proclaiming that we had been set free from the power of Satan and from death by the death and resurrection of God's Son, and brought into the kingdom of the Father. They were sent also to bring into effect this saving work that they proclaimed, by means of the sacrifice and sacraments that are the pivot of the whole life of the liturgy.

So, by baptism people are brought within the paschal mystery. Dead with Christ, buried with Christ, risen with Christ, they receive the Spirit that makes them God's adopted children, crying out: Abba, Father; and so they become the true adorers that the Father seeks.

In the same way, whenever they eat the supper of the Lord they proclaim his death until he comes. So, on the very day of Pentecost, on which the Church was manifested to the world, those who received the word of Peter were baptized. They remained steadfast in the teaching of the apostles and in the communion of the breaking of bread, praising God and enjoying the favour of all the people.

From that time onward the Church has never failed to come together to celebrate the paschal mystery, by reading what was written about him in every part of Scripture, by celebrating the Eucharist in which the victory and triumph of his death are shown forth, and also by giving thanks to God for the inexpressible gift he has given in Christ Jesus, to the praise of God's glory.[21]

WHAT TO BRING

—Sacred Crucifix and Prayer Stole

Purchase an inexpensive small crucifix and a prayer stole. Have both of these items blessed by your parish priest or chaplain. We recommend a woven Guatemalan stole common with laity in Latin America who wear them to Mass.[22] Each baptized Catholic shares in Christ's mission as "priest, prophet and king." Bring your crucifix and wear this prayer stole during your vigil. Both will become powerful holy signs of this signature spiritual event in your life.

—Your TRUE HEART materials,

—Your journal entries from the program

—A pen or two

—A Bible

—A notebook for writing

—Your favorite picture/image of Jesus and Mary—Have them with you throughout the vigil in a view from your place of prayers

— Bring some fluids and what you think you need for nourishment

—Bring a watch

---

[21] This selection is adapted from Vatican II on God's Plan of Salvation is used in the Office of Readings of the Roman Church for Saturday in the Second week of Easter. It is an excerpt from the Constitution (par. 5-6) on the Sacred Liturgy of the Second Vatican Council (1962-65).

[22] The best place to purchase one of these prayer stoles is from: http://thetreeoflifeimports.com/stoles.htm

You can also purchase a small cross from the same group that supports Fair Trade and Latin American families: http://thetreeoflifeimports.com/crosses.htm

—Dress comfortably (Dress knowing you will spend eight hours with Christ – classy but comfortable. What you wear will be determined somewhat by the weather too, so take that into consideration) Your most important element is your prayer stole.

THE HOURLY STRUCTURE

Minutes 1-5
—Kneel Silently & Listen to Your Heart
—Pray the Hail Mary & Listen to Your Heart
—Pray One of the Two Following Prayers to Affirm Christ Present in the Blessed Sacrament Before You

ANIMA CHRISTI[23]

Soul of Christ, sanctify me
Body of Christ, save me
Blood of Christ, inebriate me
Water from Christ's side, wash me
Passion of Christ, strengthen me
O good Jesus, hear me
Within your wounds hide me
Let me not be separated from You
From the hateful enemy defend me
In the hour of my death call me and bid me come to You
That I may praise You with your saints
and with your angels
Forever and ever
Amen

---

[23] Prayer from the 14th century and a favorite of St. Ignatius.

COPTIC EUCHARISTIC PRAYER[24]

Father, I believe and confess that before me is the living body which your only-begotten Son, Our Lord and Savior Jesus Christ, took from the Lady, Queen of humankind, and the Mother of God. I believe, I believe, I believe that this is in very truth the living body of Christ Jesus, present to me. Help my unbelief.

Minutes 6-40

—Spiritual Exercise (Follow what is presented for each hour)

Minutes 41-50

—Journal Exercise (Write all your short journal entries directed to Jesus Christ. For example: "Jesus, I want…..; "Jesus help me…..."; etc. Talk to Him. Ask Him for help and guidance. Let Him be Lord and Savior for you tonight.

Minutes 51-60

—Take a Break

WHAT TO EXPECT

1. Periods of consoling prayer and feeling focused
2. Periods of seeming emptiness and boredom and feeling unfocused
3. Periods of high energy and hope—feeling that you could go on forever
4. Periods of low energy and dryness—feeling that this will never end
5. Periods of clarity
6. Periods of confusion
7. Periods of fear
8. Periods of fearlessness
9. Expect everything

---

[24] Adopted from an ancient eucharist prayer for the Coptic Church.

10. Expect nothing

11. But expect that God will use this night vigil to change your life

FIRST HOUR

Minutes 1-5

—Kneel Silently & Listen to Your Heart

—Pray the Hail Mary & Listen to Your Heart

—Pray One of the Two Prayers to Affirm Christ Present in the Blessed Sacrament Before You

Minutes 6-40

—Spiritual Exercise (Read the following story, taking your time to pause and reflect as you do. There is no need to rush).

The Eucharist And Youth[25]

Life's Prospects for the Young People of Today

Some time ago I was making a long trip on a train when three young fellows of around eighteen entered into my compartment. They were accompanied by a man who was somewhat older, and after a bit, I learned that he was the director of physical education at their school.

Pedro Arrupe, High School Portrait 1923

They were tired, and after some remarks on their winning a soccer game, they dropped off to sleep, one after the other. A couple of hours later they began to speak again and to take down a good number of Cokes and orange sodas. Their conversation became lively, and they looked at me with a certain curiosity as if they were asking themselves: Who in the world is this priest? I did not join in their conversation since I had to prepare a conference which I was to give as soon as I reached my destination.

[25] Adapted from: Pedro Arrupe, *Other Apostolates Today: Selected Letters and Addresses—III*, ed. Jerome Aixala (St Louis: Institute of Jesuit Sources, 1981), 283-307. Original talk of Fr. Arrupe delivered at the Basilica of St Francis, Assisi September 6, 1979. *It is three o'clock in the afternoon. Some 1400 boys and girls of the "Eucharistic Youth Movement" have entered into the lower Basilica of St. Francis. They are members of the two senior sections of the Apostleship of Prayer for children and young men and women in Italy. Present in the present assembly there are some 950 from the groups of "Community 14", that is of boys and girls from ages 14 to 16; and 400 from the groups of "Witnesses", that is young men and women of 17 and over. So the target is what we could call today the "youth and young adults" that form the nexus of our pastoral outreach to the upcoming generation.* More from Fr. Pedro Arrupe can be found at The Arrupe Collection: https://jesuitportal.bc.edu/research/documents/the-arrupe-collection/ For information on the cause of Fr. Arrupe's canonization, visit: https://arrupe.jesuitgeneral.org/en/

At one point, when their talk seemed to be dying down, the teacher asked: "Now that you have finished school, what do you plan to do?" One of the boys answered without much thought: "I don't know. I suspect that my father will tell me; I have no thoughts about anything. Who knows? It's a tough problem. It is better that they tell me what to do. Besides, I don't care to be bothered."

The second then broke in: "I've thought a lot about it, and I don't know whether I should go into business or work in the stock market. I don't know which of these two pay the better without too much work. What I want is an easy and peaceful life. I don't care for much more."

The third seemed to be a bit ashamed. He said nothing, and it looked as if he wanted to avoid giving an answer. The two others looked at him with some perplexity, and after a few seconds the teacher asked him: "And you, Frank, what are you going to do?" "To tell the truth, I'm not sure myself. I have been thinking about going for some years to some spot in the Third World to see its greatest need. I could then be a help to many who are suffering in it."

The eyes of the other two started to pop out as if to ask: "Frank, are you crazy?" The teacher then queried him: "How did you get that idea?" "I don't know," Frank replied a bit embarrassed, "but the idea has been floating around in my head for some months. Do you think it a crazy idea?" "No, not crazy, just a bit strange. Still, Frank, I really admire you."

At this, I was no longer able to keep quiet. In a low voice I said what I was thinking: "It's great, Frank. Follow that tugging of your heart since it must be a heart of gold." My four traveling companions looked at me and then began to speak about soccer.

I also let go of the topic, but I began to think how these three young people clearly manifested different attitudes shared by today's youth:

There are those who are not much on thinking. They let themselves be carried along by circumstances. They don't want to be bothered. And why? You live very well if you have no worries.

There are those who have no other ambition than to make money, and this with the least effort possible. They are self-centered at heart: "I go my way, and others can think what they want." They believe that they can find their happiness in

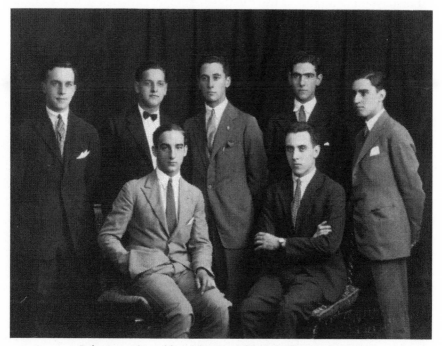

Pedro Arrupe (second from left top) with friends in Bilbao, Spain ca 1924

money. They let themselves be carried off by appearances, by what they see in ads, by the fascination of the world of entertainment. But there are also those of noble heart who are moved by a desire to be of help to others, to console those who are afflicted, to be of service to others even at the cost of personal sacrifices.

My encounter with Christ

Dear members of the Youths' Eucharistic Movement, you have invited me to share in this festival of yours; and I would like to speak with each one of you

231

about the plans which you are cherishing in your hearts for your future life. Are you waiting for someone to tell you what you should do? Do you want to make money most of all in order to be happy? Do you feel a longing to serve your brothers and sisters? There is perhaps no one of you that has ideas that are firmly fixed, but certainly you are more or less inclined to one of these three general tendencies.

To you, to your questions, and to your expectations, I am today telling you in all simplicity what I have myself experienced in meeting Jesus Christ. A few weeks ago in Rome, a group of pilgrims, boys and girls, came to pay me a visit after the Wednesday audience of the pope. At one point, one of the younger of the group asked me point blank: "Why did you become a Jesuit?" — "Because I believed that it was my vocation."

— "And why did you believe it was your vocation?" — "Because I felt that God was calling me." — "And why was He calling you?" — "Well, the Lord wished to have another who would consecrate himself completely to Him, and He chose me" — "What did you think?" — "I thought that it would cost me much to abandon my career as a doctor, but that by becoming a Jesuit I could labor even more for others. I would be able to cure not only bodies but also souls."

Another boy broke in: "Father, I have heard that different Jesuits have been killed. It must be a rather risky vocation." — "You are right. Six Jesuits have been killed in Rhodesia, four in Lebanon, one in Chad, two in Latin America." — "Why don't you defend yourselves? Why don't you use weapons?" — "There's not even a thought of that. We want to be of service to all without discrimination.

We live to serve. If we are killed for our service, it is a great honor for us!" — "But if you are hated and you let yourselves be killed, you have to have a lot of courage. I don't get it." — "Right you are, but the Lord gives one strength since it is done for Him, and it is He who gives us strength." — "So," the boy exclaimed in amazement, and his face showed that he had failed to understand; and the same expression could be seen on the faces of the rest, who were listening in silence.

I then tried to explain myself: "Look at it this way. We Jesuits became such and continue to be such simply out of our enthusiasm for Jesus Christ and from our desire to work for Him and for others. Jesus Christ is most faithful. He does not abandon those who are dedicated to His service. Jesus Christ lived two thousand years ago, but he still lives today in the Eucharist and in the depths of our hearts.

One of those present suddenly exclaimed: "What? I'm getting less now than I did before!" The rest began to laugh.

I believe that this conversation, simple and straight-forward as it was, revealed a whole series of feelings, questions, and attitudes that are prevalent among young people today. And I am certain that you who have already become familiar with Jesus Christ will understand me better than the boy who said: "What? I'm getting less now than I did before!" I am certain that you will understand me.

One Same Jesus: the Jesus of the Gospel and the Jesus of the Eucharist
It is a fact that Jesus Christ, especially in the Eucharist, is a source of energy for all: for us Jesuits, for you young people, for all, since Jesus Christ is present and lives for us in the Eucharist. He becomes our Friend, our Ideal, our Model, our Strength, our Way. You should know Jesus Christ. The more you know Him, the more you will love Him, since He is in addition to being God—nothing less—He is also a perfect man, one who is both simple and congenial.

During the course of history there have been, and even today there are, many leaders, many individuals who represent different ideologies and who seek to attract us and to convince us that it is worth the effort to follow them and to dedicate ourselves to their cause, but there is no one who can be compared in this regard with Jesus Christ, even from a distance.

Those who dealt with him said: "No one has ever spoken as this man." "You have the words of eternal life." "Let us follow him and stay with him." "For him I have accepted the loss of everything, and I look at everything as so much rubbish if only I can have Christ."

What can we do to gain an ever better knowledge of Jesus Christ? It is really very simple. In the Gospels, we have a true picture of the historical Jesus, of the Jesus as he lived in Palestine. And in the Eucharist, we have Jesus Christ living today in the midst of us. In neither case can we see him with our eyes, but the Gospel narrative is the word of God which gives vitality to what is said. When we read the Gospels we realize that the person of Jesus, who lived two thousand years ago, is still alive; and we feel Him very close to us.

It is as though Jesus of Nazareth continues to live now as He did then. And on the other hand, the Eucharist is the same Body and Blood of the risen Christ. He is alive and present though hidden under the sacramental species. He lets himself be perceived. He speaks to us. He inspires and strengthens us.

Saint Teresa of Lisieux arrived at such a living faith in the presence of Jesus Christ in the Eucharist that she used to say: "If they told me that Jesus was in the house next to mine, I would not go to see Him since I already have Him with me in the tabernacle and He visits me daily in Holy Communion. I do not have greater faith in the eyes of my face than in those of my faith. The eyes of the body can be deceived, but not those of faith."

Pedro Arrupe as a Jesuit Novice

By bringing together the two figures, that of the Gospel and that of the Eucharist, we shall obtain the precise image of what Jesus was and is today. Do you really wish to know Jesus Christ, to be transformed by Him? Read the Gospel before the tabernacle, receive Him in Holy Communion, ask Him with His disciples: "Lord, teach us! Lord, we do not understand what you are saying. Explain it to us!"

There is no doubt that in this way each one of us can obtain a true concept of Jesus, even though He is endowed with an infinite richness which no one can completely comprehend, assimilate, or imitate. Each one of us understands or imitates some aspects of the figure of our Lord. All the saints have sought to imitate Jesus and they are all different from each other starting with St. Paul who is different from St. Peter.

Nevertheless, we should all seek to make for ourselves an image of Jesus Christ and to grasp as surely as we can His personality. The path which we follow in our lives should be one that brings us ever closer and ever more dedicated to Him, the Jesus of the Gospel and the Jesus of the Eucharist, who is the same and only Jesus, the Jesus who has risen and is alive, who loves us and seeks us as He does the whole of humankind.

To explain what I want to say, I shall relate some of my own experiences which were connected with the Eucharist and in which I recognize the hand of the Lord who led me and still leads me in my way of life. But I am sure that you also can reflect on your own experience up till now and on the way in which the Lord is guiding you on the path of your life.

Minutes 41-50

—Journal Exercise for Hour One

Ponder each of the following questions. Only reflect on one question at a time and don't read ahead. Write the one thing that seems most significant to you at this point in your life from each question. Only move ahead when the Spirit prompts you, taking time to fully explore what your heart is experiencing. Remember to write your short entries directly to Jesus. If you don't complete the reflection/answer process, you will have time to do so at the beginning of the next hour. So relax and reflect peacefull.

✠ Imagine you are going to tell your closest friend about this story. What would be the first thing you shared with them? Ponder. Write in your journal no more than two sentences as a response, clarifying what you would share and why you want to share it.

✠ Fr. Arrupe described three types of responses people can have to making life-choices (see below). Pretending you don't have to tell anyone else but Christ, present to you in the Eucharist, write in your journal which type of person you are *most* like at this time in your life, and why. Write what type of person you want to become, and why. Finally, compose a two-sentence prayer to Christ asking for the help to become your True Heart.

a. *There are those who are not much on thinking. They let themselves be carried along by circumstances. They don't want to be bothered. And why? You live very well if you have no worries.*

b. *There are those who have no other ambition than to make money, and this with the least effort possible. They are self-centered at heart: "I go my way, and others* can think what they want." They believe that they can find their happiness in money. They let themselves be carried off by appearances, by what they see in ads, by the fascination of the world of entertainment.

c. But there are also those of noble heart who are moved by a desire to be of help to others, to console those who are afflicted, to be of service to others even at the cost of personal sacrifices.

✠   Fr. Arrupe described the honor of serving others, even at the cost of one's life. Speak to Christ present to you in the Blessed Sacrament and tell him the one thing that would be worth the price of your own life. Ponder with Christ. Write that one thing in your journal with words that begin: "Jesus, I would give my life for….." "Jesus, I would give it because……"

✠   Fr. Arrupe said: *Do you really wish to know Jesus Christ, to be transformed by Him? Read the Gospel before the tabernacle, receive Him in Holy Communion, ask Him with His disciples: "Lord, teach us! Lord, we do not understand what you are saying. Explain it to us!"* Do you want to know Christ and be transformed by him?

✠   He is present to you. Speak to and tell him how you want to know him? How do you want to be transformed by him? Write in your journal one sentence on what you told Christ about each.

✠   Fr. Arrupe affirms that each saint in the history of the Church is different. Yet, each was transformed by the same Christ. Who is the same person who walked the earth and who is Present in the Blessed Sacrament Before You. Ponder if you desire to be a saint. Ask Jesus if he can make you one and how you would be remembered by history. What do you hear? Write what you hear from Jesus in your journal.

Minutes 51-60

—Take a Break

SECOND HOUR

Minutes 1-5

—Kneel Silently & Listen to Your Heart

—Pray the Hail Mary & Listen to Your Heart

—Pray One of the Prayers to Affirm Christ Present in the Blessed Sacrament Before You

Minutes 6-40

—Spiritual Exercise: If you did not complete the reflection/answers from the previous hour, do those first. When complete, continue reading the story, taking your time to pause and reflect as you do. There is no need to rush.

Jesus, the Worker of Miracles, the Healer of the Ill,
Is Calling Me and Is Sending Me on a Mission
The first of my Eucharist experiences was closely connected with my vocation as a Jesuit, the same vocation about which those boys asked me as I observed earlier. The experience was that of a miracle which I saw at Lourdes during the procession of the Blessed Sacrament on the esplanade that lies in front of the basilica.

Some weeks after the death of my father I had gone to Lourdes with my family since we wished to spend the summer in quiet, peaceful, and spiritual surroundings. It was the middle of August. I stayed at Lourdes for a whole month; and since I was a medical student, I was able to obtain a special permission to study closely the sick who came seeking a cure.

Fr. Pedro Arrupe's First Mass 1936

One day I was in the esplanade with my sisters a little before the procession of the Blessed Sacrament. A cart pushed by a woman of middle age passed in front of us. One of my sisters exclaimed: "Look at that poor boy in the cart." It was a young man of around twenty, all twisted and contorted by polio.

His mother was reciting the rosary in a loud voice and from time to time she would say with a sigh: "*Maria Santissima (Holy Mary)*, help us." It was a truly moving sight, and I remembered the plea which the sick turned towards Jesus: "Lord, cleanse me from this leprosy!" She hastened to take her place in the row which the bishop was to pass carrying the Blessed Sacrament in a monstrance.

The moment came when the bishop was to bless the young man with the Host. He looked at the monstrance with the same faith with which the paralytic mentioned in the Gospel must have looked at Jesus. After the bishop had made the sign of the cross with the Blessed Sacrament, the young man rose cured from the cart, as the crowd filled with joy cried out: "Miracle! Miracle!"

Thanks to the special permission which I had, I was later able to assist at the medical examinations. The Lord had truly cured him. There is no need to tell you what I felt and my state of mind at that moment. I had come from the Faculty of Medicine in Madrid, where I had had so many professors (some truly renowned) and so many companions who had no faith and who always ridiculed miracles. But I had been an eyewitness of a true miracle worked by Jesus Christ in the Eucharist, by that same Jesus Christ who had, during the course of His life, cured so many who were ill and paralytic.

I was filled with an immense joy. I seemed to be standing by the side of Jesus; and as I sensed His almighty power, the world that stood around me began to appear extremely small. I returned to Madrid. My books fell from my hands. The lessons, the experiments which had so thrilled me before now seemed so very empty. My comrades asked me: "What's happening to you this year? You are like one who has been stunned!"

Yes, I was like one stunned by that impression which every day grew more disconcerting. The one thing that remained fixed in my mind and in my heart was the image of the Host as it was raised in benediction and of the paralyzed boy who had leapt from his cart. Three months later I entered the novitiate of the Society of Jesus in Loyola, Spain.

The teaching of our Lord was the same as that of the Gospel. Through his miracles and His teaching, He awakened in me a faith and love for Him so that He could finally say: "Leave everything and follow me!" The Lord of the monstrance was the same Lord as that of the Gospel. His powers were the same, and His wishes were as they had then been: "May the workers, who are few, become more numerous since the harvest is great."

Once this voice is heard today as it was twenty centuries ago, it cannot be forgotten. One is, of course, free to follow it or not, but one with judgment or reason, as St. Ignatius of Loyola says, will end with following it. There is no doubt that the force which goes forth from Jesus in the Eucharist, and which went forth on that unforgettable afternoon at Lourdes, is the same that went forth from Jesus in Gospel times.

That experience at Lourdes was a repetition of what the contemporaries of Jesus saw when the crowds surrounded him and he cured all (Mt 9:18; 14:14; Mk 2:13; 3:20; Lk 5:17-26, etc.). Certainly, it is a question of the same Jesus, now hidden under the sacramental species, but with the same love and the same power. These are experiences which leave an indelible trace and bring it about that we also can say with the apostle: "That which we have seen and heard and touched of the Word of life, that is what we preach to you." (1 Jn 1:1).

Our vocation as Jesuits is essentially missionary. It is thus normal that a Jesuit should go to one of those countries known as a mission country. From the time that I became a Jesuit in 1927 until 1937, when I was destined to Japan, I had continuously asked to be sent there, since it seemed to me that it was the place for me. This conviction had its origins in a deep feeling within me. But the Lord had confirmed it in circumstances connected with the Eucharist.

Once when I had just finished serving Mass for our superior in the novitiate, his name was Cesareo Ibero, I told him that I had received a negative answer from the General of the Society of Jesus to my request to be sent to Japan. The rector, who was descending from the altar where he had finished celebrating Mass, told me: "You will go to Japan."

At that moment I felt as if the Lord who had been offered upon the altar had said through the lips of my superior: "Your vocation is to go to Japan, millions of souls are waiting there for you. That is the field of your apostolate." It was Jesus who told me from that hour what would be officially decided ten years later. It was the same Jesus who called His disciples from among others (Jn 1:40-45) so that He might personally send each one of them on his own way.

I also remember that in October 1938, when I was sailing from Seattle to Yokohama, that as I was celebrating Mass alone in the cabin of the ship, I recalled that incident when the rector of Loyola spoke to me when I was still a young Jesuit student. At that moment, when I was now a priest, I held in my hands, in the Host which I had myself consecrated, Him who had destined me for that same country in which another great Jesuit, St. Francis Xavier, had begun to preach the Gospel four hundred years before.

There in my hands was that Savior who had said to his apostles: "Go and preach to all people; I shall be with you till the end of time." On the ship, I experienced great joy and was inspired with the thought of the work which I was about to begin in Japan. It seemed to me that Jesus Himself, whom I held each day in my hands, was teaching me as He had taught the crowds from the prow of the ship on the lake of Tiberias (Mt 13:1-3).

It seemed to me that it was that same wisdom which had then spoken in parables that had spoken also to me, but in a manner which I could not fully understand as yet: It was that "for the moment you cannot understand" (Jn 16:12), as Jesus told His disciples. There were, in fact, things that would have then been too hard and difficult for me, but He who was speaking to me was the same Master who had said: "I will give you rest" (Mt 11:28).

Minutes 41-50
—Journal Exercise for Hour Two
Ponder each of the following questions. Only reflect on one question at a time and don't read ahead. Write the one thing that seems most significant to you at this point in your life from each question. Only move ahead when the Spirit prompts

you, taking time to fully explore what your heart is experiencing. Remember to direct your short responses directly to Jesus. If you don't complete the reflection/answer process, you will have time to do so at the beginning of the next hour. So relax and reflect peacefully.

✠ Pedro's family went to Lourdes after his father died. He was a medical student at the time and was permitted to investigate reported miraculous healings. This suggests that he might have believed them to be possible or that he was skeptical and wanted to verify to prove otherwise. Which do you think was his main motive before he witnessed the miracle, and why? Ponder. Then write two sentences first describing which motive seems most true to you and second, why you choose that one.

✠ Pedro witnessed a truly miraculous healing of a profoundly crippled young man. First, it brought him joy. As the weeks progressed, he became stunned and disconcerted. His friends noticed it. Why do you think he went from joy to being stunned and confused? Talk to Jesus about it and ponder. Write one sentence on why you believe this change came over Pedro.

✠ Pedro's witnessing a miracle cure through the Blessed Sacrament moved him from wanting to be a doctor to wanting to work for Jesus. It does not matter that the "call" was as a priest but that he felt "called." Have you ever felt "called" by Jesus to do something? What was it?

✠ What miracle would it take to make you want to follow Jesus? Ponder. Can you ask Jesus for this miracle? Write what miracle you want and what it would do for you.

✠ Pedro continued to have experiences of being confirmed and "called" that coincided with experiences of Christ present in the Blessed Sacrament. Including your time tonight, can you recall any events in your life connected with Christ present in the Blessed Sacrament where you were "called and/or confirmed" in something? Ponder. Write that experience in one sentence if yes.

Minutes 51-60

—Take a Break

THIRD HOUR

Minutes 1-5

—Kneel Silently & Listen to Your Heart

—Pray the Hail Mary & Listen to Your Heart

—Pray One of the Prayers to Affirm Christ Present in the Blessed Sacrament Before You

Minutes 6-40

—Spiritual Exercise (If you did not complete the reflection/answers from the previous hour, do those first. When complete, continue reading the story, taking your time to pause and reflect as you do. There is no need to rush).

The Body and Blood of Jesus for the World

The mission which the Lord entrusts to us, though it has its origins in a personal encounter with Him, is always open to others, to the entire world, since the Lord has shed His blood "for the multitude," that is for all. Every Mass is a Mass for the world and in the world. I remember the Mass which I celebrated at the top of the famous Mount Fujiyama, at a height of more than 11,000 feet.

I had climbed it with one of my religious brothers. At that time it was made almost entirely on foot. One could only go on horseback to a height of about 3,300 feet. It was necessary to reach the summit by four in the morning to be able to see the marvelous panorama since by six the peak was covered with clouds and could no longer be seen.

Fr. Arrupe elevating the Host at sunrise during Mass on Mount Fuji 1939

We arrived on time and celebrated Mass in the most complete solitude. It was shortly after I arrived in Japan. I was living through the first impressions of a new environment and my mind was bubbling with a great number of projects for the conversion of the whole of Japan. We had climbed Fujiyama so that we might be able to offer to the Eternal Father the Sacrifice of the Immaculate Lamb for the salvation of all Japan at the highest point in all that country.

The climb had been most tiring since we had to hasten in order to arrive on time. Several times we thought of Abraham and Isaac as they climbed a mountain to offer their sacrifice. Once we had reached the top, the sight of the rising sun was stupendous. It raised our spirits and disposed them for the celebration of the Holy Sacrifice. Till then I had never celebrated Mass in such conditions. Above us, the blue sky expanded like the cupola of an immense temple—brilliant and majestic.

Before us, were all the people of Japan, at that time some eighty million who did not know God. My mind ranged out beyond the lofty vaulting of the sky to the throne of the divine Majesty, the seat of the Blessed Trinity. I seemed to see the holy city of the heavenly Jerusalem. I seemed to see Jesus Christ and with Him St. Francis Xavier, the first apostle of Japan, whose hair had become white in the course of a few months because of the sufferings he had to endure. I also was being confronted by that same Japan as Xavier had been. The future was entirely unknown. If I had then known how much I would have to suffer, my hands would have trembled as I raised the sacred Host.

On that summit so near to heaven it seemed to me that I understood better the mission which God had entrusted to me. I descended from it with a renewed enthusiasm. That Eucharist had made me feel the grandeur of the everlasting God and universal Lord. At the same time, I had felt that I was an "assistant," a sharer in the labor of Jesus Christ in the great redemptive mission entrusted to Him by His Father. I could repeat with more sincerity and conviction the words of Isaiah: "Here I am, send me" (Is 6:8) or those of St. Francis Xavier: "I am! Behold me."

Our Lord also, as is told in the Gospel, went up a mountain with His disciples and was transfigured before them (cf Mt 17:4). I also experienced the longing to remain there and not to leave so that I might continue to relish those heavenly moments, as St. Peter had when he exclaimed, "It is good for us to be here. If you wish I shall prepare three tabernacles one for you, one for Moses (my companion, Moses Domenzáin, bore this same name), and one for Elias." (Mark 9:5).

That same Jesus who had filled St. Peter with joy and admiration, so much so that he had adored Him "falling with his face to the earth" (Mt 17:6), had also shown Himself to me in the sublime sight of our Eucharist—the sacred Host, illuminated by the white light of the rising sun seemed to be transfigured before my eyes, and I believed that I heard with St. Peter the voice of the Lord which said to me: "Have no fear" (cf Mt 17:7). It was a word most necessary for me as I was descending from those heights to the harsh life that was waiting for me during those years in Japan. How many things can Our Lord teach and make one feel in a single Mass?

From this, it is almost natural for me to pass on to another remembrance of the Eucharist, to a Mass celebrated in very different circumstances from those just mentioned. This Mass taught me how Jesus, who suffers and dies for us, can bring about His plan of salvation through the mysterious ways of sorrow and suffering.

The atomic bomb had exploded at 8:10 on August 6, destroying the whole of Hiroshima, reducing it to ashes and killing at one blow eighty thousand people. Our house was one of the few that remained standing, even though it was badly damaged. There were no windows or doors left, all had been torn away by the violent wind caused by the explosion. We turned our house into a hospital and assembled there around two hundred who were injured in order to nurse and assist them.

The explosion had occurred on the sixth of August. On the following day, the seventh, at five in the morning before beginning the work of helping the wounded and burying the dead, I celebrated Mass in our house. It is certain that in the most tragic moments we feel nearest to God and the importance of His assistance. Actually, the external surroundings were not much adapted for fostering devotion during the celebration of the Mass.

The chapel, half destroyed, was packed full of those who had been injured. They were lying on the floor close to each other and they were obviously suffering from the torments of their pains. I began the Mass as best I could in the midst of that crowd which did not have the least idea of what was taking place upon the altar. They were all pagans and had never seen a Mass.

I cannot forget the frightful impression I had when I turned towards them at the opening "The Lord Be With You." (Mass was then said with one's back to the congregation) and saw that sight from the altar. I was unable to move and remained as if I were paralyzed with my arms stretched out as I contemplated that human tragedy: human knowledge, technical advance used for the destruction of the human race. All looked at me with eyes filled with anxiety, with desperation, as though expecting that some consolation would come to them from the altar. It was a frightful scene! Within a few minutes, there would descend upon the altar the one of whom John the Baptist had said: "There is one in the midst of you whom you do not know" (Jn 1:26).

I had never sensed before so greatly the solitude of the pagan ignorance of Jesus Christ. Here was their Savior, the One who had given His life for them, but they "did not know who was in the midst of them" (cf Jn I:26). I was the only one who knew. From my lips there spontaneously went forth a prayer for those who had had the savage cruelty to launch the atomic bomb: "Lord, pardon them, since they do not know what they are doing." and for those who were lying before me, tortured by their pains: "Lord, grant them faith so that they may see; give them the strength to endure their pains."

When I lifted the Host before those torn and mangled bodies there rose from my heart: "My Lord and my God: have compassion on this flock without a shepherd!" (Mt 9:36; Mk 6:34). Lord, may they believe in You. Remember that they also must come to know You (1 Tim 2:4).

Certainly from that Host and from that altar there poured forth torrents of grace. Six months later, when all, already cured, had left our house (only two persons died), many of them had received baptism, and all had learned that Christian charity can have compassion, can assist, can give a consolation that is above all human comfort, can give a peace that helps one to smile in the midst of pain and to pardon those who had made us suffer so much.

Such Masses as these are moments replete with a sacramental intuition which arrives at understanding what is so difficult or so impossible to understand without faith, that is, the value of suffering, the beauty and sublimity of the sacrifice of charity.

Minutes 41-50
—Journal Exercise for Hour Three

Ponder each of the following questions. Only reflect on one question at a time and don't read ahead. Write the one thing that seems most significant to you at this point in your life from each question. Only move ahead when the Spirit prompts you, taking time to fully explore what your heart is experiencing. Remember to direct your short responses directly to Jesus. If you don't complete the reflection/answer process, you will have time to do so at the beginning of the next hour. So relax and reflect peacefully.

✠ Fr. Arrupe climbed one of the iconic mountains of the world, Fuji, to celebrate Holy Mass at its summit. His faith told him Christ would be present in that Mass. In "sight" before him and his Jesuit companion, were all the people in Japan who did not know Christ. Do you know Christ Jesus well enough that you would feel passionate about bringing knowledge of Him to people? Ponder. Talk to the Lord and write to him one or two sentences. First, ask Him to give you the kind of knowledge of Him that would make you want to "tell the world" about Him. Second, talk with Jesus about with whom would you want most to share knowledge of Him.

✠ Fr. Arrupe received a powerful grace at his Mass on Mount Fuji. Yet he would later discover that suffering would enter his life and the people he came to bring the Good News. As you are present to Christ in the Blessed Sacrament, what suffering in the world do you "see" with Him that causes you to be shaken? Ponder. Write down in one sentence that form of suffering.

✠ Many of those to whom Fr. Arrupe nursed back to health after the nuclear blast became Catholic Christians. He said they discovered: *that Christian charity can have compassion, can assist, can give a consolation that is above all human comfort, can give a peace that helps one to smile in the midst of pain and to pardon those who had made us suffer so much.* Suffering is not the end of the story. Hope is. Look out into the world again with Christ and see with new eyes those you thought above. Ponder. In a sentence or two, ask Jesus to bring them peace, healing and the grace to forgive any who caused their suffering.

Minutes 51-60
—Take a Break

FOURTH HOUR

Minutes 1-5

—Kneel Silently & Listen to Your Heart

—Pray the Hail Mary & Listen to Your Heart

—Pray One of the Two Prayers to Affirm Christ Present in the Blessed Sacrament Before You

Minutes 6-40

—Spiritual Exercise (If you did not complete the reflection/answers from the previous hour, do those first. When complete, continue reading the story, taking your time to pause and reflect as you do. There is no need to rush).

Jesus Friend and Consoler

Another type of Eucharistic experience is that which shows us the value that the Most Blessed Sacrament has for us when we have been in intimate and prolonged contact with Him during our life and we sense the lack of this sacrament when we are not able to receive it. At such a time we appreciate the great role which Jesus, our friend, companion, and consoler has in our life if we have been and are habitually nourished by the Eucharist.

I remember a Japanese girl of around eighteen whom I had baptized three or four years earlier and who had become a fervent Christian. Every day she received Communion at the six-thirty Mass in the morning, which she promptly attended every day.

One day after the explosion of the atomic bomb, I was passing through streets clogged with masses of ruins of every kind. On the spot where her house had formerly stood, I found a kind of hut supported by some poles and covered with pieces of tin. I went up to it. A wall about a foot and half high marked off a place within its interior. I tried to enter but an unbearable stench repelled me. The young Christian woman, her name was Nakamura, was lying stretched out on a rough table raised a bit above the ground. Her arms and legs were extended and covered with some burned rags. Her four limbs had become along their whole length a single sore from which pus was oozing and falling down upon and penetrating the earth.

Her burned flesh seemed to be little else but bones and wounds.

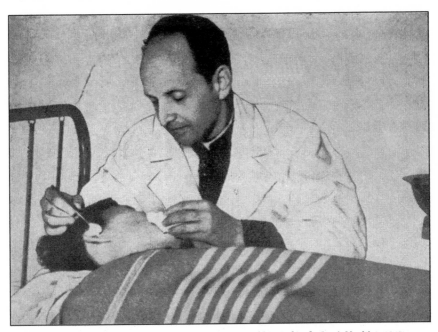

Fr. Arrupe helping a Hiroshima victim at the improvised hospital in the Jesuit Novitiate 1945

She had been in this state for fifteen days, without being able to take care of herself or clean herself, and she had only eaten a little rice which her father, who was also seriously injured, gave her. Her back was already one gangrenous mass since she had not been able to change her position. When I sought to clean her burns, I found that the muscles were rotten and transformed into pus that left a hollow into which my hand entered and at the bottom of which was a mass of worms.

Appalled by such a terrible sight, I remained without speaking. After a little, Nakamura opened her eyes and when she saw me near, and smiling at her, she looked at me with two tears in her eyes and sought to give me her hand which was only a purulent stump and she said to me with a tone that I shall never forget: "Father, have you brought me Communion?"

What a Communion that was, so different from that which I had given her each day for so many years! Forgetting all her sufferings, all her desires for physical relief, Nakamura asked me for what she had continued to desire for two weeks, from the day on which the atomic bomb had exploded. She asked for the Eucharist, for Jesus Christ, her great consoler, to whom she had months earlier offered her body and soul to work for the poor as a religious.

I would have given anything to have been able to hear her speak of that experience of her lack of the Eucharist and of her joy at receiving it after so much suffering. Never before had I experienced such a request, from one who had been so cruelly reduced to a "wound and ulcer," nor such a Viaticum[26] received with such an intense desire. Nakamura San died soon after, but she had been able to receive and embrace Jesus whom she had loved so much and who was anxiously waiting to receive her forever in His home in heaven.

The absence of Jesus is something like that which Martha felt when after the death of Lazarus she said to Jesus: "Lord, if you had been here, my brother would

---

[26] The Blessed Eucharist—Communion—given to a person in danger of death.

255

not have died" (Jn 11:32). It was precisely then that Jesus performed one of the greatest miracles of His public life. Like Martha, Nakamura also was able to feel that Jesus, though absent exteriorly, had not abandoned her and that He would come to meet her again to take her to Himself and make her completely happy for all eternity.

I have frequently thought of that scene of Nakamura San. How much it taught me! The value of the Eucharist for souls who have truly experienced it, the desire to receive it that causes one to forget every other kind of suffering and need, the joy of receiving it, all the greater the longer that one has been deprived of it, the strength that Christ gives us under the sacramental species, communicating to us His love and His incomparable joy.

Fr. Arrupe (top right) with his Catholic catechists and catechism students, Yamaguchi, 1941

A religious who, because of her work with the poorest people of Peru, could only assist at Mass every six weeks, since she had to remain far from a place of worship, told me: "It is just in this situation that I feel more what the Eucharist means for me." If we must leave our Lord to serve the souls of others, He makes

Himself felt more deeply even in His physical absence since He is always living in the depth of our soul.

I myself personally experienced this deep sense of pain for the lack of the Eucharist during the thirty-three days that I was imprisoned in Japan, but there was also at the same time a feeling of the faithful and consoling presence of Our Lord. The enemies of Christianity had made a thousand accusations against me. They were angry, since they saw that while they were trying to put obstacles in the way to conversions, a good number of young people were turning to the Church and were receiving baptism.

The war broke out in Japan on the feast of the Immaculate Conception, 1941, with the attack of Pearl Harbor. The military police immediately put me in jail, in a cell with an area of four square meters. I did not know why they had put me there, and I was not told why for a long time, and only at the end of my confinement.

I passed the days and nights in the cold of December entirely alone and without a bed, or table, or anything else but a mat on which to sleep. I was tormented by my uncertainty on why I had been imprisoned. This provoked a kind of self-torture because of the presumptions, suspicions, and fears that I had done something that could have been a source of harm to others. But I was above all tortured by not being able to say Mass, at not being able to receive the Eucharist.

What loneliness there was! I then appreciated what the Eucharist means to a priest, to a Jesuit, for whom the Mass and the tabernacle are the very center of his life. I saw myself dirty, unshaven, famished, and chilled to the bone without being able to talk with anyone. But I felt even more anguish for my Christians who were perhaps suffering because of me. And above all, there was no Mass. How much I learned then! I believe that it was the month in which I learned the most in all my life. Alone as I was, I learned the knowledge of silence, of loneliness, of harsh and severe poverty, the interior conversation with "the guest of the soul," who had never shown Himself to be more "sweet" than then.

During those hours, those days, those weeks of silence and reflection I understood in a more illuminating and consoling way the words of Christ: "Remember what I have told you: a servant is not more important than his master. If they have persecuted me, they will also persecute you" (Jn 15:20).

I was interrogated for thirty-six hours in a row. I was asked matters that were very touchy to answer and I was myself astonished by the "wisdom" and the fitness of my replies. It was a proof of the saying of the Gospel: "Do not be concerned about what you must say to defend yourselves. I shall give you the right words and I shall give you such wisdom that all your adversaries will not be able to resist and much less defeat you" (Lk 21:14-15).

When my sufferings were becoming more cruel, I experienced a moment of great consolation. It was Christmas night. My mind went back to so many happy Christmases, to the three Masses which I was able to celebrate that night. What remembrances filled my mind! But none of all this was now possible. I was alone, without Mass. Instead of Christmas, it seemed more like Good Friday!

Just then when my Christmas was being changed into the Passion and that blessed night into a sad Gethsemani, I heard a strange sound near one of the windows. It was the soft murmur of many voices which with muted accents sought to escape detection. I began to listen. If any of you have been in prison waiting for a sentence, you would appreciate the anxiety with which I followed those sounds which were now of themselves becoming an immediate source of suspicion. Such are the fears that one feels within the four walls where one is detained.

Suddenly, above the murmur that was reaching me, there arose a soft, sweet, consoling Christmas carol, one of the songs which I had myself taught to my

Christians. I was unable to contain myself. I burst into tears. They were my Christians who, heedless of the danger of being themselves imprisoned, had come to console me, to console their Shimpu Sama (their priest), who was away that Christmas night which till now we had always celebrated with such great joy. What a contrast between that thoughtfulness and the injustice of senseless imprisonment!

The song with those accents and inflections which are not taught or learned poured forth from a touching kindness and sincere affection. It lasted for a few minutes, then there was silence again. They had gone and I was left to myself. But our spirits remained united at the altar on which soon after would descend Jesus. I felt that He also descended into my heart, and that night I made the best spiritual Communion of all my life.

From then on the Eucharist became for me something new and different. I sought never to lose it. The moment when one loses something is also the moment in which its worth is best known. And so, my dear young friends, the Eucharist is a treasure, a great treasure which the Heart of Christ was able to give to humankind.

There is still another incident that has been most instructive in my life and which made me understand more fully the intimacy which we should have with Jesus in the Eucharist and that the simpler one's manner of prayer is the more profound it becomes.

I was once in Yamaguchi in charge of a group of young women and men. Among these was a woman of about twenty who, without any show, went to the chapel and remained on her knees before the tabernacle, at times for hours on end. She seemed to be absorbed, as she remained there motionless. I was struck by the fact that though she was a young woman like all the others, very charming and cheerful, she went to the chapel with such persistence, though she was living together with her companions who held her in the highest esteem.

Fr. Pedro Arrupe at Hiroshima hearing in 1945

One day I met her, or rather, I made it a point to meet her, as she was leaving the chapel. We began to speak as usual and our conversation fell upon her constant and long visits to the Blessed Sacrament. She had hardly given me the chance to speak about this when I asked her: "And what do you do in so much time before the tabernacle?" Without hesitation, as if she had already prepared her answer, she told me: "Nothing." "What? Nothing?" I insisted. "Does it seem possible to you to remain so long without doing anything?"

This sharpening of my request, which wiped out all possibility of doubt, seemed to upset her a little. This time she was a little more slow in answering me. At last she said: "What do I do before the tabernacle? Well, I am there." Then she was silent again. And we took up again our ordinary conversation.

She seemed to have said nothing, at least nothing particular. But in reality she had not concealed anything and had said everything with a word replete with content. In a single word she had condensed the whole meaning of being present before the Lord: "To be," as Mary, the sister of Lazarus, was at the feet of the Lord (Lk 19:39), or as His Mother stood at the foot of the cross.

They also were there. Hours of friendship, hours of intimacy, during which nothing is lost and it seems that nothing is said, since that which is given is everything—one's whole being. Unfortunately, there are too few who understand the value of this "being" at the feet of the Master in the Eucharist, of this apparent loss of time with Jesus.

Would you like to have some good advice from me? Look upon Jesus as your friend, as your confidant. Learn to go and see Him, to visit Him, to "remain" with Him, and you will see how many things you will learn. It is a wisdom which He alone can give you, the true knowledge which makes people wise, holy, and even happy. All that we need for our life is gradually attained with a pouring forth from heart to heart. "Tell me with whom you associate, and I shall tell you who you are." If you go with Jesus, if you remain with Jesus, you will certainly become, yourself, another Jesus.

Minutes 41-50

—Journal Exercise for Hour Four

Ponder each of the following questions. Only reflect on one question at a time and don't read ahead. Write the one thing that seems most significant to you at this point in your life from each question. Only move ahead when the Spirit prompts you, taking time to fully explore what your heart is experiencing. Remember to direct your short responses directly to Jesus. If you don't complete the reflection/answer process, you will have time to do so at the beginning of the next hour. So relax and reflect peacefully.

✠ Nakamura, who was suffering and on the point of death from radiation poisoning, smiled at Fr. Arrupe and asked if he came to bring her Communion. Talk with Jesus about what kind and depth of love someone can have to ignore suffering and focus only on His presence to them in the Blessed Sacrament. Ponder. In your own words, ask Jesus if you can know His love this deeply. Write what you asked Him in one sentence.

✠ Fr. Arrupe was imprisoned and suffering extreme anxiety not knowing what crime he caused. But mostly he was suffering because he was prevented from saying Mass and offering it for his "new" Christians. His friends risked their lives to sing him a Christmas carol and he wept for gratitude. Have you ever suffered extreme anxiety and suddenly someone risks helping you and brought you joy? Ponder, Ask Jesus if he would make it possible for you to take a risk to help someone in great need. If you know what risk you might take, write for the grace to make it happen. Write it in a single sentence request to Jesus.

✠ A young woman who would spend hours in front of the Blessed Sacrament caught Fr. Arrupe's attention. Yet when he pressed her what she did with such great amounts of time, all she said was, "I am there." You have "been here" before Christ in a similar way for about four hours. Fr. Arrupe suggests you become another Jesus by "being with" him. You have another four hours ahead of you. Tell Jesus you are happy just being with him. In a single sentence, ask him to give you the will to take time each week to simply be with him in the presence of the Blessed Sacrament, so that you become more like him.

Minutes 51-60
—Take a Break

FIFTH HOUR

Minutes 1-5

—Kneel Silently & Listen to Your Heart

—Pray the Hail Mary & Listen to Your Heart

—Pray One of the Prayers to Affirm Christ Present in the Blessed Sacrament Before You

Minutes 6-40

—Spiritual Exercise (If you did not complete the reflection/answers from the previous hour, do those first. When complete, continue reading the story, taking your time to pause and reflect as you do. There is no need to rush).

Jesus has a Special Love for the Poor

Certainly Jesus, the same Jesus of the Gospel and of Eucharist, can say profound and precious things to those who have cultivated for a long time an intimacy with him, but we should not think that he cannot speak to all people, even though they are living in the most difficult conditions and in utter poverty. Rather, it is precisely that Jesus who gave His blood for them, that can find secret and wonderful ways for reaching their hearts.

A few years ago I was visiting a Jesuit province in Latin America. I was invited, with some timidity, to celebrate a Mass in a suburb, in a "favela," the poorest in the region, as they told me. There were around a hundred thousand people living there in the midst of mud. The town had been built along the side of a depression and became almost completely flooded whenever it rained.

I readily accepted since I know from experience that visits to the poor are most instructive: they do much good for the poor, but one also learns much from them.

The Mass was held in a small structure all patched together and open. Since there was no door, cats and dogs came and went without any problem. The Mass began. The songs were accompanied by a guitar which was strummed by one who was not exactly an expert, but the results seemed marvelous to me.

The words were as follows: "To love is to give oneself, to forget oneself, by seeking that which can make another happy." And they continued: "How beautiful it is to live for love, how great it is to have to give. To give joy and happiness, to give oneself, this is love." "If you love as you love yourself, and give yourself for others, you will see that there is no egoism which you cannot conquer. How beautiful it is to live for love."

Gradually as the song went on, I felt a knot in my throat and I had to force myself to continue with the Mass. Those people, who seemed to have nothing, were ready to give themselves to share their joy and happiness.

When we arrived at the consecration and I raised the Host in the midst of an absolute silence, I perceived the joy of the Lord who remains with His beloved. As Jesus says: "He has sent me to bring the good news to the poor" (Lk 4:18), "Blessed are the poor in spirit" (Mt 5:3).

Soon after, when I was distributing Communion and was looking at their faces, dry, hard, and tanned by the sun, I noticed that large tears like pearls were running down many of them. They were meeting Jesus, their only consolation. My hands trembled.

I gave them a brief homily in dialogue. They told me things which are heard with difficulty in lofty discourses. They were very simple things but at once human and sublime. One old woman asked me: "You're the superior of these priests, aren't you? Well, 'Señor,' thanks a thousand times since your Jesuit priests have given us the great treasure which we lacked, and of which we have the greatest need, the Holy Mass."

One young man said openly: "Señor padre, you should know that we are very thankful since these priests have taught us to love our enemies. One week ago I had prepared a knife to kill a comrade whom I hated much, but after I heard the priest explain the Gospel, I went and bought an ice cream and gave it to my enemy."

Fr. Arrupe's posture for reading and praying 1964.

At the end, a big fellow, whose terrible looks could have inspired fear, told me: "Come to my house. I have something to honor you." I remained uncertain, not knowing whether I should accept or not, but the priest who was accompanying me said: "Go with him, father; the people are very good." I went to his house, which was a half falling-down shack. He made me sit on a rickety chair. From where I was seated the sun could be seen as it was setting.

The fellow said to me: "Señor, see how beautiful it is!" And we remained silent for some minutes. The sun disappeared. The man added: "I did not know how to thank you for all that you have done for us. I have nothing to give you, but I thought that you would like to see this sunset. It pleased you, didn't it? Good evening." He then gave me his hand. As I was leaving I thought: "I have met very few hearts that are so kind."

I was about to leave that street when a small woman very poorly dressed came up. She kissed my hand, looked at me and said with words filled with emotion: "Father, pray for me and for my children. I was at that beautiful Mass which you celebrated. I am running home. But I have nothing to give to my nine children. Pray to the Lord for me: He must help us." And she disappeared almost running in the direction of her house.

I learned many things with one Mass among the poor. How different from the great receptions of the leaders of this world!

Minutes 41-50
—Journal Exercise for Hour Five
Ponder each of the following questions. Only reflect on one question at a time and don't read ahead. Write the one thing that seems most significant to you at this point in your life from each question. Only move ahead when the Spirit prompts you, taking time to fully explore what your heart is experiencing. Remember to direct your short responses directly to Jesus. If you don't complete the reflection/answer process, you will have time to do so at the beginning of the next hour. So relax and reflect peacefully.

✠ Fr. Arrupe described a situation where in extreme poverty, people had a most profound faith. Have you had an experience of being with people who have next to nothing whose faith in God and Jesus is rock solid? Ponder. If you can remember a situation, write it down in a single sentence addressed to Jesus. "Jesus, I remember...etc."

✠ The poor who received communion from Fr. Arrupe had tears running down there faces, so moved that the Lord was coming to them. Jesus who is truly present in the Blessed Sacrament must have also been overjoyed to bring such hope to the poorest of the poor. Contemplate Jesus' joy at a Mass like this where he is able to touch and be present to those with nothing. Ponder his joy and ask Jesus what he felt. Listen. Write what you "heard" in a single sentence. Remember that one and same Jesus is present to you, too.

✠ A woman who had nothing to feed her nine children asked Fr. Arrupe to ask God to help her. She believed God could help her because of the "beautiful Mass" she experienced with Fr. Arrupe. Contemplate a situation in your own life or the world that seems impossible to resolve, and ask Jesus to make it work. Ponder. Describe in two sentences the situation and tell Jesus you "believe" he can resolve it.

✠ The presence of Christ transformed a man's hatred and desire to kill into a desire to be reconciled Has your intense anger toward "an enemy" of yours ever been similarly transformed? Ponder. Write to Jesus in a sentence or two what you remember.

✠ The most precious gift the fearful looking man could offer Fr. Arrupe was a chair at his house to watch the sunset. When can you remember being so moved by the beauty of creation that you stopped and gave thanks? Ponder. Tell Jesus in a single sentence what you saw and thank Him because "all things were made through Him and for Him."

Minutes 51-60
—Take a Break

SIXTH HOUR

Minutes 1-5

—Kneel Silently & Listen to Your Heart

—Pray the Hail Mary & Listen to Your Heart

—Pray One of the Two Prayers to Affirm Christ Present in the Blessed Sacrament Before You

Minutes 6-40

—Spiritual Exercise for Hour Six

(If you did not complete the reflection/answers from the previous hour, do those first. When complete, continue reading the story, taking your time to pause and reflect as you do. There is no need to rush).

The "Eucharist Person," the "New" Person Modeled upon Jesus Christ

I could go on telling you of other experiences which I have had, but the time does not permit it. Let us, therefore, sum up what I have sought to tell you up till now. Our Lord, through contact with Him in the Eucharist, has entered into the project of my life.

He has revealed Himself to me in different and ever new ways and He has transformed my plan of life into his own plan of life, the plan which He made known in the Gospel, for He, the Jesus of the Gospel and the Jesus of the Eucharist are the same Jesus risen from the dead and living.

268

He, the worker of miracles, the *Almighty Healer of the sick*, met me on the esplanade of Lourdes in the Host that was blessing the ill. He *chose me* and *sent me personally with an apostolic mission* to continue His work, when the superior of Loyola at the end of his Mass, confirmed me in my aspiration to ask for the mission in Japan, and when during the Mass on the ship, He made me feel that I was near the apostles whom He sent into all the world and to St. Francis Xavier.

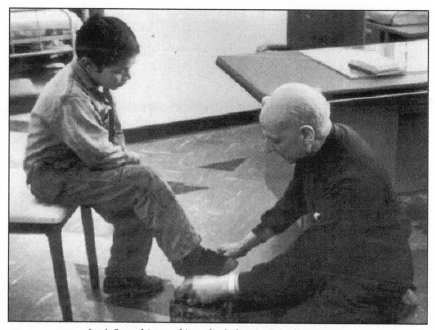

Jesuit General Arrupe shines a boy's shoes in Quito, Ecuador 1971

He, the *Anointed-Victim* who offers Himself upon the cross to His Father for the salvation of the world, for all the people who do not yet know Him, at one with all those who suffer, offered Himself in my hands on the highest peak in Japan and in the midst of those who had been tortured and wounded by the atomic bomb. And again, He has always shown Himself to me as a most faithful friend. He, the *great consoler in suffering*, fulfilled the hunger and the longing of Nakamura as she was dying and rent with pain.

He, the *true and sole companion*, able to remain united with us even in the most absolute solitude, never abandoned me in the days when I was in prison.

He, *the friend who communicates Himself* in silence to those who "remain" near him as to that girl in Yamaguchi. He who *has a special love for the poor* and knows how to fill them with joy and to bless them with great gifts that are hidden to us, as to those Christians of the Mass in the "favela" of Latin America.

We should now reflect on all this and strive to draw some practical results for our own personal lives. I shall limit myself to some brief points. Continue to ponder them.

The central ideal which your movement presents to you is that of "a person of the Eucharist," that is, of a person who, like Jesus, carries to the very end the plan of the Father, dedicating yourself totally to others, letting your heart be broken for them on a universal level open to all the world, to all people. This person of the Eucharist is the new person, the person who wishes to build a new world with Jesus. In the midst of the present culture with its advances and limitations, you wish in fact to be new, that is to be modern among those who are modern. The problem consists in knowing the criteria of this newness and in remaining constant to it.

If the newness is measured by the style of dress or of hair, by "fashion," by entertainment, the use of drugs, by confrontations and by the recourse to violence, I believe that you will certainly not be "the newest" young men and women.

But the true criterion of what is new is that which is described by St. Paul. According to him, to be old persons means to be slaves to sin, to have that hardness of spirit of one who has lost his moral sense, who lets one's conduct become disordered and delivers oneself over to the unbridled practice of every kind of impurity (cf Eph 4:22-24). According to this criterion, many young people who claim to be "modern," and "new," are precisely those who are most "old."

A person who is truly "new" is the one created by God after the model of Jesus Christ "in justice and in holiness' holiness' (Eph 4:24), "renewed (by God) to bring you to perfect knowledge and to make you like to Him who has created you" (Col3 :9-10) "with sentiments of mercy, kindness, humility, patience, and sweetness, supporting one another, pardoning one another…And above all may you have love, which is the bond of perfection" (Col 3:12).

This perfection in charity brings a great joy, the serenity which is the fruit of the Spirit. Because of this, you should always be the most cheerful of those who are young, with the joy and the smile most solid and profound, that joy which, as St. John says, no one can take from you (Jn 16:22).

The criteria for recognizing people who are "new," are those which were spoken of the first and true "new" man, Jesus of Nazareth, the Christ, the man-God. He is that charming friend who spoke in such a way that one who heard Him exclaimed: "No one has spoken as this man" (Jn 7:49), "He did everything well" (Mk 7:37), "To whom shall we go? You have the words of eternal life" (Jn 6:69), "Let us also go with him to die" (Jn 1lI:16). He is that friend who has so given Himself for us that He offered His life in the terrible tortures of the cross, but who, having risen, lives forever, not only at the right hand of the Father in heaven, but also much closer to us in the Eucharist.

The Eucharist gives some very precious characteristics to Christ's complete giving of Himself. They are a source of inspiration for your life as "Witnesses," and they renew you each day, making you ever more "new" and ever more "women and men of the Eucharist."

Jesus Christ becomes our food in the Eucharist, a new food, so that He may be united in the most intimate measure possible with us and to give us new strength to plan and build a new world. Jesus Christ in the Eucharist, hidden under the sacramental species, remains near us in the tabernacle as a faithful friend to encourage us and to teach us to be "new" as he was.

Strive to become intimate with, and to obtain a knowledge of Jesus Christ in the Eucharist. May He be the force which moves you along the path of the new world. Christians should not only be new for themselves but also witnesses, leaders, precursors of the truest modernity, heralds of Christ, always new and always modern.

All this that I wish to say to you can be summed up in your being friends of Christ, but true friends. He has chosen us as His friends; "You are my friends" (Jn 15:14). Now we are those who must choose Him as our friend, but as a true friend, as our best friend. And to be converted to Him, to be more closely united with him, to be identified with Him, to continue His life in ours, there is no more direct route than that which passes through the Eucharist.

Lord, You have before You this group of young men and women who have heard Your invitation: "If you wish to be perfect, sell all that you have, and give it to the poor, then, come and follow me" (Mt 19:21). They long to be faithful to You, to follow You wherever you go and to give their lives for You. They are so filled with enthusiasm for You that they say, as Ittai, one of King David's chief captains and most faithful friends said to King David: "By Yahweh and your life, my lord king, where my lord king is, living or dead, there also will your servant be" (2 Sam 15:21).

True "people of the Eucharist," who are engaged in building a new world, are those who follow their Lord wherever he goes and who, to follow their Lord wherever he goes and who, to follow him, are nourished by his Body and Blood, and are thus transformed into "other Christs." From here, you should leave with a heart on fire, on fire with the love of Christ, who is the only one who can transform the self-centeredness of the heart of stone of the old person into the person of today.

Pope John Paul II & Fr. Arrupe, Jesuit General 1980

Minutes 41-50

—Journal Exercise for Hour Six

Ponder each of the following questions. Only reflect on one question at a time and don't read ahead. Write the one thing that seems most significant to you at this point in your life from each question. Only move ahead when the Spirit prompts you, taking time to fully explore what your heart is experiencing. Remember to direct your short responses directly to Jesus. If you don't complete the reflection/answer process, you will have time to do so at the beginning of the next hour. So relax and reflect peacefully.

✠ To be a "new person" or a True Heart, Fr. Arrupe offers that fashion, entertainment and/or ideologies are really not going to help a person achieve the goal. Talk with Jesus about what challenges you face in conforming to the "fashions of the day" in order to fit in and to be accepted. Ponder. What are the specific challenges? In two sentences, write the main one(s) and ask for His help to overcome the temptation conform and instead to be a "new" True Heart—a truly "modern" person.

✠ Fr. Arrupe said: *He (Jesus) the true and sole companion, able to remain united with us even in the most absolute solitude, never abandoned me in the days when I was in prison. He, the friend who communicates Himself in silence*

273

to those who "remain" near him as to that girl in Yamaguchi. He who has a special love for the poor and knows how to fill them with joy and to bless them with great gifts that are hidden to us, as to those Christians of the Mass in the "favela" of Latin America.

Write in a sentence or two what specific desires you have to serve others when you read these reflections.

✠ Fr. Arrupe said: *Jesus Christ becomes our food in the Eucharist, a new food, so that He may be united in the most intimate measure possible with us and to give us new strength to plan and build a new world. Jesus Christ in the Eucharist, hidden under the sacramental species, remains near us in the tabernacle as a faithful friend to encourage us and to teach us to be "new" as he was.*

How many visits per week and/or how much time do you feel called to spend in quiet prayer with Christ each week in His presence in the Blessed Sacrament? Write down what you deisre. Then in a next sentence, ask Jesus, present before you, to give you the grace to act on this desire closing with: "Thank you, Jesus, for hearing my prayer!"

Minutes 51-60
—Take a Break

SEVENTH HOUR

Minutes 1-5

—Kneel Silently & Listen to Your Heart

—Pray the Hail Mary & Listen to Your Heart

—Pray One of the Two Prayers to Affirm Christ Present in the Blessed Sacrament Before You

Minutes 6-40

—Spiritual Exercise

FIRST PART: The Lord Jesus, present to you in the Blessed Sacrament, desires to be your friend. He wants you to join Him in his work to heal the world. He knows there is something that only you can do for Him and He desires to lead you to the knowledge of this life mission. Pray the Triple Colloquy of St. Ignatius for the graces to be open to this knowledge. Take as much time as you want for these three conversations.

TRIPLE COLLOQUY OF SAINT IGNATIUS

First Colloquy, or conversation, will be with Mary. Speak with Mary, using your own words asking her to obtain from her Son <u>the grace to follow her Son selflessly in every act and decision of your life</u>. Pray to know more specifically what path will bring you to your True Heart—to being truly "new" and truly "modern." When you finish this conversation, pray the *Hail Mary* slowly, thinking of the words and the person to whom you are praying.

Fr. Arrupe after his stroke with Mother Theresa of Calcutta ca 1982

Second Colloquy, or conversation, will be with Jesus. Speak directly to Jesus, asking him to request his Father for the same graces as above, i.e., using your own words, He will request from His Father the grace for you to follow Him in every act and decision of your life. Pray to know more specifically what path will bring you to your True Heart—to being truly "new" and truly "modern." When you finish your conversation, pray the *Anima Christi* slowly, thinking of the words and the person to whom you are praying.

Soul of Christ, sanctify me. Body of Christ, save me. Blood of Christ, fill me. Water from the side of Christ wash me. Passion of Christ, strengthen me. O Good Jesus, hear me. Within thy wounds, hide me. Permit me not to be separated from thee. From the wicked foe, defend me. At the hour of my death, call me, and bid me come to thee that with thy saints I may praise thee forever and ever. Amen.

Third Colloquy, or conversation, will be with God the Father. Ask the Father directly in your own words to give you the graces so you may follow His Son. Ask the Father for the grace for you to follow Jesus in every act and decision of your life. Pray to know more specifically what path will bring you to your True Heart—to being truly "new" and truly "modern." When you finish, pray the *Our Father*, thinking of the words and the person to whom you are praying.

SECOND PART: You have asked the Blessed Mother, Jesus and the Father for graces to know how best to find your True Heart. You have done this in the presence of Jesus in the Blessed Sacrament. Tell Jesus now: "I believe you have heard my prayers and that you will, in time, reveal all to me."

Minutes 41-50

—Journal Exercise for Hour Seven
Go back now and review all that you have written in your journal entries this vigil thus far. Read the questions and read what you spoke to Jesus in your responses. Ask for the grace "to see" and "to hear" how the Holy Spirit is working in your heart this night by "understanding with the eyes of faith" what your heart—your True Heart—is revealing to you. When you are done, write what immediately comes to your heart when you read the prompts below.

✠ Jesus, the challenge where I struggle most to believe you will be real and present to me in my life is...

✠ Jesus, what I see most about my life that gives me hope is.....

✠ Jesus when I look at the world, what causes me the greatest distress is....

✠ Jesus, I would like to help people most by....

✠ Jesus, what it means for me to sell all I have and follow you is....

✠ Jesus, if one day I might be known as one of your saints, I would be honored to be remembered most for....

✠ Jesus....(speak to Christ from your heart)

Minutes 51-60
—Take a Break

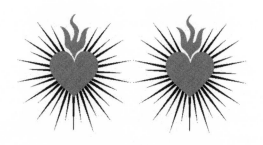

FINAL HOUR

Minutes 1-5

—Kneel Silently & Listen to Your Heart

—Pray the Hail Mary & Listen to Your Heart

—Pray One of the Prayers to Affirm Christ Present in the Blessed Sacrament Before You

Minutes 6-40

—Spiritual Exercise

—Write a personal dedication prayer that describes your desire to serve Jesus and His Kingdom. A template is provided below. You may no clue as to the shape that call will take. Yet, offer to serve Christ with your whole life by the path or vocation that will set your free you and make you a True Heart.

For you to be authentically most who you are—a True Heart—will be your path to holiness.

Make yourself available for the work of this Kingdom here on earth, so you can praise Him forever in the Eternal Kingdom of the Blessed. Your dedication should be no longer than 5-8 sentences! Something short enough that you can pray it briefly each day from here on out.

Praying the Ignatian Examen opens us to the spiritual world. It heightens consciousness so we can discern the authentic from the inauthentic in all of our thoughts, word and deeds. St. Ignatius prayed it hourly. His Constitutions require Jesuits pray it twice daily. It is the Spiritual Exercises in miniature and opens one to live life as a True Heart for the Greater Glory of God.

For the end of the True Heart journey and the close of the Night Vigil, you are creating your own unique version of this key, strategic prayer of discernment. Praying this will open you to Divine inspiration on a daily basis and "drag you" into miracles of grace!

Reflect on the prayer movements below and add your own conclusion to each of the Creation, Presence, Memory, Mercy and Eternity prayers.

CREATION

I believe God created everything in love and for love; I ask for heartfelt knowledge of God's love for me, and for gratitude for the general and particular graces of this day. (Add a sentence or two to personalize this grace for yourself).

PRESENCE

I believe God is present in each moment and event of my life, and I ask for the grace to awaken, see and feel where and how, especially in this present moment. (Add a sentence or two to personalize this grace for yourself).

MEMORY

I believe every violation of love committed by me and against me is in my memory, and I ask God to reveal them to me, especially those that have manifested themselves today, so I can be healed. (Add a sentence or two to personalize this grace for yourself).

MERCY

I believe that forgiveness is the only path to healing and illumination. I beg for the grace of forgiveness, and the grace to forgive, especially for the general and particular failures of this day, and from my past. (Add a sentence or two to personalize this grace for yourself).

ETERNITY

I believe the grace of forgiveness opens my heart, making my every thought, word and deed bear fruit that endures to eternity. I ask that everything in my life serve Christ's Great Work of Reconciliation. (Add a sentence or two to personalize this grace for yourself).[27]

✠ Pray your unique version of the True Heart Prayer and then pray *Foundations Prayer* afterward. Pause at the end of the Foundations Prayer and listen to your heart before moving to the next step.

FOUNDATIONS PRAYER

For and through whom everything was made,
Is Christ Jesus. I live because he loves me.
To praise and serve him alone with all my mind, heart,
and strength is my freedom—my only freedom.
I shall not prejudice any path in following him:
for I can praise him equally in my health and sickness.
I can distinguish myself in service to his Kingdom with
great wealth, modest means, or having
nothing at all to call my own.

---

[27] Ignatian Examen Adapted by William M. Watson, S.J.

He is the anchor of my joy and peace

Whether I am disgraced or lauded.

In his all-embracing love I taste eternity,

whether my days are numbered great or small.

Christ Jesus alone is the treasure of my heart.

I shall ever listen for his call,

and follow unreservedly.

For in everything I can love and praise him,

and find my eternal joy.

Amen.[28]

✠　Pray your unique version of the True Heart Prayer and then pray the two Psalms below afterward. Pause at the end of the Psalms and listen to your heart before moving to the next step.

PSALM 114-115

When Israel came forth from Egypt,

the house of Jacob from an alien people,

Judah became God's sanctuary,

Israel, God's domain.

The sea saw and fled;

the Jordan turned back.

The mountains skipped like rams;

the hills, like lambs.

Why was it, sea, that you fled?

Jordan, that you turned back?

---

[28] A paraphrase by William Watson, SJ, of the First Principle and Foundation of St. Ignatius from the Spiritual Exercises.

Mountains, that you skipped like rams?
You hills, like lambs?
Tremble, earth, before the Lord,
before the God of Jacob,
Who turned the rock into pools of water,
flint into a flowing spring.

Not to us, LORD, not to us
but to your name give glory
because of your mercy and faithfulness.
Why should the nations say,
"Where is their God?"
Our God is in heaven
and does whatever he wills.

Their idols are silver and gold,
the work of human hands.
They have mouths but do not speak,
eyes but do not see.
They have ears but do not hear,
noses but do not smell.
They have hands but do not feel,
feet but do not walk;
they produce no sound from their throats.
Their makers will be like them,
and anyone who trusts in them.

The house of Israel trusts in the LORD,
who is their help and shield.
The house of Aaron trusts in the LORD,
who is their help and shield.

Those who fear the LORD trust in the LORD,

who is their help and shield.

The LORD remembers us and will bless us,

will bless the house of Israel,

will bless the house of Aaron,

Will bless those who fear the LORD,

small and great alike.

May the LORD increase your number,

yours and your descendants.

May you be blessed by the LORD,

maker of heaven and earth.

The heavens belong to the LORD,

but he has given the earth to the children of Adam.

The dead do not praise the LORD,

not all those go down into silence.

It is we who bless the LORD,

both now and forever.

Hallelujah![29]

✠   Pray your unique version of the True Heart Prayer and then pray the *Teach Me Your Ways* and the *Personal Prayer of Pedro Arrupe* afterward. Pause at the end of both prayers and listen to your heart before moving to the next step.

TEACH ME YOUR WAYS

Teach me your way of looking at people:

as you glanced at Peter after his denial,

as you penetrated the heart of the rich young man

and the hearts of your disciples.

---

[29] Psalm 114-115.

I would like to meet you as you really are,
since your image changes those with whom you
come into contact.
Remember John the Baptist's first meeting with you?
And the centurion's feeling of unworthiness?
And the amazement of all those who saw miracles
and other wonders?
How you impressed your disciples,
the rabble in the Garden of Olives,
Pilate and his wife
and the centurion at the foot of the cross. . . .
I would like to hear and be impressed
by your manner of speaking,
listening, for example, to your discourse in the
synagogue in Capharnaum
or the Sermon on the Mount where your audience
felt you "taught as one who has authority."[30]

PERSONAL PRAYER OF PEDRO ARRUPE

Grant me, O Lord, to see everything now with new eyes,
to discern and test the spirits
that help me read the signs of the times,
to relish the things that are yours, and to communicate them to others.
Give me the clarity of understanding that you gave Ignatius.

---

[30] Prayer of Pedro Arrupe.

✠   Pray your unique version of the True Heart Prayer and then pray So Many Things afterward. Pause at the end of So Many Things and listen to your heart before moving to the next step.

SO MANY THINGS

To each one of you in particular
I would love to say –
tantas cosas: so much, really.
From our young people I ask
that they live in the presence of God
and grow in holiness,
as the best preparation for the future.
Let them surrender to the will of God,
at once so awesome and so familiar.
With those who are
at the peak of their apostolic activity,
I plead that they do not

burn themselves out.

Let them find a proper balance

by centering their lives on God,

– not on their work –

with an eye to the needs of the world,

and a thought for the millions

that do not know God

or behave as if they did not.

All are called to know and serve God.

What a wonderful mission

has been entrusted to us:

to bring all to the knowledge

and love of Christ![31]

✠   Pray your unique version of the True Heart Prayer and then pray *I Tasted and I Saw* afterward. Pause at the end of *I Tasted and I Saw* and listen to your heart before moving to the next step.

I TASTED AND I SAW

Eternal God, eternal Trinity, you have made the blood of Christ so precious through his sharing in your divine nature. You are a mystery as deep as the sea; the more I search, the more I find, and the more I find the more I search for you. But I can never be satisfied; what I receive will ever leave me desiring more. When you fill my soul I have an even greater hunger, and I grow more famished for your light. I desire above all to see you, the true light, as you really are.

---

[31] A Prayer of Fr. Arrupe for Young Adults: He added at the end. *On those of my age I urge openness: let us learn what must be done now, and do it with a will. For this I offer to the Lord what is left of my life, my prayers and the sufferings imposed by my ailments.*

I have tasted and seen the depth of your mystery and the beauty of your creation with the light of my understanding. I have clothed myself with your likeness and have seen what I shall be. Eternal Father, you have given me a share in your power and the wisdom that Christ claims as his own, and your Holy Spirit has given me the desire to love you. You are my Creator, eternal Trinity, and I am your creature. You have made of me a new creation in the blood of your Son, and I know that you are moved with love at the beauty of your creation, for you have enlightened me.

Eternal Trinity, Godhead, mystery deep as the sea, you could give me no greater gift than the gift of yourself. For you are a fire ever burning and never consumed, which itself consumes all the selfish love that fills my being. Yes, you are a fire that takes away the coldness, illuminates the mind with its light and causes me to know your truth. By this light, reflected as it were in a mirror, I recognise that you are the highest good, one we can neither comprehend nor fathom. And I know that you are beauty and wisdom itself. The food of angels, you gave yourself to man in the fire of your love.

You are the garment which covers our nakedness, and in our hunger you are a satisfying food, for you are sweetness and in you there is no taste of bitterness, O triune God![32]

✠   Pray your unique version of the True Heart Prayer and then pray *O Most Holy Virgin* afterward. Pause at the end of *O Most Holy Virgin* and listen to your heart before moving to the next step.

O MOST HOLY VIRGIN

O most holy Virgin, Mother of Jesus and my mother,

---

[32] From the dialogue On Divine Providence (Chapter 167) by Saint Catherine of Siena, virgin and doctor.

I kneel in prayer at your feet in the very presence of your Son.

I join my voice to all the angels and saints in heaven.

With them, I join in praising you for your "yes" to the Angel Gabriel in giving

birth to Jesus. Please intercede that I might

be able this day to say "yes" in following your Son.

Dear Mary, help me with your powerful guidance in all my undertakings and

toils. Protect me from all enemies and console me in all my trials.

Bring it to pass, that I might live all my life, shaped by the Way, Truth and

Light of Christ until I reach the Kingdom of the Eternal Father.

Amen. [33]

✠   Pray your unique version of the True Heart Prayer and then pray *Dedication to the Heart of Christ* afterwards. Pause at the end of *Dedication to the Heart of Christ* and listen to your heart before moving to the next step.

DEDICATION TO THE HEART OF CHRIST

Heavenly Father, as Ignatius prayed in the small chapel of La Storta, you

granted by an extraordinary grace to answer the request which he had been

begging of you for a long time through the intercession of Our Lady:

To be placed with your Son.

In your words to him you assured him of your support:

"I shall be with you".

You asked Jesus carrying his cross to take him as your servant.

This he did. He turned to Ignatius with those unforgettable words:

"It is my will that you serve us."

As a follower of Jesus, I address to you the same prayer,

---

[33] The Dedication prayer to Mary is adapted from the traditional solemn consecration of the Society of Jesus to the Immaculate Heart of Mary.

asking to be placed with your Son and to serve "under the banner of the Cross"

where Jesus is nailed out of his infinite love.

His side is pierced and his heart is opened

As a sign of his love for me and for all people.

I now consecrate myself to the Heart of Jesus

And promise you my allegiance.

Please give me the grace to serve your Son

with the same spirit and same intensity as Ignatius.

Through the intercession of the Virgin Mary who received the prayer of

Ignatius, and before the Cross where Jesus Christ gives to us the treasures of

His open heart, through Him and in Him,

I say from the very depths of my being:

Take, O Lord, and receive all my liberty, my memory,

My understanding, and my entire heart.

Whatever I have or hold, you have given me.

I give it back to you and surrender it wholly to be governed by your heart.

Give me only your love and your grace,

And I am rich enough, for I need or desire nothing else. [34]

Closing Minutes – The Rest of Your Life

—Journal Exercise

Write in your journal the three most significant things you desire to remember for the rest of your life from this night vigil. When you finish, kneel and pray the Glory Be.

---

[34] The Dedication Prayer to the Sacred Heart is adapted from Pedro Arrupe's prayer of the Consecration to the Heart of Christ.

GLORY BE

Glory be to the Father
To the Son,
And to the Holy Spirit.
As it was in the beginning,
Is now,
And ever shall be.
World without end.
AMEN!

THE REST OF YOUR LIFE

Abide in Me
A Daily Relationship with Christ as Savior,
Divine Physician and Lord of All

I invite you to pray with the first few verses of chapter fifteen from the Gospel of St. John. Take as many minutes, hours or days as you wish to pray with St. John. There is no hurry.

I am the true vine, and my Father is the vinedresser. Every branch of mine that bears no fruit, he takes away, and every branch that does bear fruit he prunes, that it may bear more fruit. You are already made clean by the word which I have spoken to you. Abide in me, and I in you. As the branch cannot bear fruit by itself, unless it abides in the vine, neither can you, unless you abide in me. I am the vine, you are the branches. He who abides in me, and I in him, he it is that bears much fruit, for apart from me you can do nothing.

If a man does not abide in me, he is cast forth as a branch and withers; and the branches are gathered, thrown into the fire and burned. If you abide in me, and my words abide in you, ask whatever you will, and it shall be done for you. By this my Father is glorified, that you bear much fruit, and so prove to be my disciples. As the Father has loved me, so have I loved you; abide in my love. If you keep my commandments, you will abide in my love, just as I have kept my Father's commandments and abide in his love. These things I have spoken to you, that my joy may be in you, and that your joy may be full. (Jn 15: 4-11)

The Ignatian *Examen* that inspires *TRUE HEART* prayer became an active part of my Jesuit life in 1994. Having entered the Society of Jesus in 1973, I had already lived for twenty years as a Jesuit—eight of those years as a priest. My practice of this prayer was inconstant for many years. By most measures, one could say that I *had* a Christian vocation. I mean this in much the same way that one looking at a Catholic married couple with children or a single person doing service work would agree that each of these persons *have* a Christian vocation.

A life of prayer and daily Mass, a yearly eight-day retreat, and a fair amount of *theological living* (faith-oriented reading plus lots of God/Church conversations) made me feel I *had* a real religious life. And I did. The question for me had become instead: was I fully *living* a Christian vocation? The answer to that is much more complex. For simplicity's sake, let me say that I have learned more clearly that a Christian vocation is not equivalent to simply belonging to a religious order. To use an analogy, a *Christian marriage* is different from *being Catholic and married with children.*

My Christian vocation requires that I daily open myself to Jesus and allow my actions, emotions, desires, loves, hurts, fears, and plans (especially my precious plans), to be shared with and shaped by Jesus' influence. Sharing means that I submit myself to Jesus and let Him have a say in what I am doing and who I am daily becoming, what I hold on to and what I relinquish. Acting in a Christian way means that I no longer belong to myself. Rather, I belong to Christ.

Some good friends of mine who have been married for several years recently shared with me one of the biggest adjustments they have had to make as a result of being married. They can no longer make plans in blissful isolation but have to consult with each other about practically every aspect of their lives. This consultative sharing can be both a joy and an annoyance.

Each one is called out of the prison of their own ego and invited to love, sacrifice, and make adjustments so that the other can grow and flourish. We really grow when we are called out of ourselves. But there is joy in sharing intimately in the life of the Beloved. We are created for the joy of sharing intimately in the life of the other. We are made in the image and likeness of God who *is relationship*.

A Christian vocation requires an intimate relationship with Christ. It requires making this relationship a priority on a *daily* basis. *TRUE HEART* prayer, more than any other spiritual discipline I have encountered in my forty years in religious life, brings me face-to-face with Christ in a relationship that calls me out of myself. It is the most effective path that has enabled me to be true to the man and priest that God desires me to be.

It is not always easy and I do not want to minimize the challenge it has been in terms of my honesty and openness. It is a joy and an annoyance for exactly the same reasons as any serious relational commitment. I have had moments of aggravation and difficulty in praying *TRUE HEART*. I have also experienced times when I did not want to pray because I knew I would be confronted with things I would prefer to ignore.

Here is a typical example. Some time ago, I was struggling internally with someone who, I judged, had wronged me. I was hurt, frustrated, and upset from what I perceived to be an injustice against myself. I discovered I was not at all upset when this person experienced misfortunes, for I felt this person *deserved* it. In prayer, I was not speaking with Jesus about this person. Instead, I found myself rehearsing conversations in my head about how I had been wronged. My focus was on myself.

One day I was awakened to my lack of Christian charity. Instinctively I understood that I needed to bring my feelings about this person to Jesus and yet, I resisted. A part of my heart wanted to simply rehearse my justified hurts. It took several *TRUE HEART* prayer periods for me to begin to speak *from my heart* to Christ about what I was feeling.

The *insight* that I needed to reach out and forgive this person came in a split-second. I was also able to accept some of the fault lines in my own personality which may have contributed to the initial difficulties. It is amazing how that clarity comes with honesty. This was a *graced* experience!

However, upon leaving the time of *TRUE HEART* prayer, a new inspiration took hold. Perhaps it is unwise to forgive? I could lose ground. The re-emerging frustration and darkened spirit—the counter-inspiration—accompanying this new inspiration was in *marked* contrast to the peacefulness I had experienced previously in the time of *TRUE HEART* prayer. In testing the spiritual inspirations, it was clear which inspiration was from the Divine-Inspirer and which inspiration was from the counter-inspirer.

Honestly, I was strongly tempted to *ignore* the truth of my spiritual discernment and go with the refusal to forgive. But I was being invited by God to *disarm*. I was invited to be vulnerable. It was an invitation to greater spiritual freedom, the freedom that Ignatius calls *detachment*. Freedom *sounds* good, but it is not something we always really want.

This event was a wake-up call because it clearly presented the difficult choice of forgiveness. It may sound odd but it gave me the conviction that Jesus is interested in *everything* I am doing. Every thought, word and deed I have is important to Christ. He wants to be part of everything I experience. *TRUE HEART*, prayed faithfully, has made me aware of what *being in relationship* with Jesus means.

I feel the effects of the surrender that is necessary for a real relationship with Jesus, and I feel it in a particularly powerful way twice a day. I have chosen to make spiritual surrender the center of my Jesuit life. And praying *TRUE HEART* prayer has revealed how many areas of my daily life I keep off-limits from Christ.

A strong intellectual tradition is a characteristic of the Society of Jesus; it is a good in and of itself. But there is something that Ignatius wanted Jesuits to value above learning: virtue, the spiritual life, and the surrender of our will and our hearts to Christ. The human gifts we cultivate only reach their fruitfulness in light of a well-grounded spiritual life. In Section Ten of the Jesuit Constitutions, entitled "How the Whole Body of the Society is to be Preserved and Increased in its Well-being," Ignatius says:

Thus it appears that care should be taken in general that all the members of the Society devote themselves to the solid and perfect virtues and to spiritual pursuits, and attach greater importance to them than to learning and other natural and human gifts. For these interior gifts are necessary to make those exterior means efficacious for the end which is being sought.
(Part X [813] 2.)

This advice is written for Jesuits, and for the care and growth of the Society of Jesus. Yet it offers good pragmatic Ignatian wisdom that is applicable to any vocation or situation in the Church. Human gifts and qualities reach their perfection and the height of their potency when the bearer of those gifts and/or qualities is grafted to the vine of Christ—when they surrender to Christ.

This holds true for the talents of the athlete, the intellectual acumen of the college student, the artistic skills of the singer or architect, the healing gifts of the doctor or nurse, the ministry of religious and priests, the leadership skills of the politician and the professional business person, and the love of husband and wife for each other and their children.

The personal decision I face daily—twice daily—is how much of my life will I allow to be grafted onto the vine of Christ? How much will I allow myself to *abide* in His Love? Jesus must have been looking at grapevines when He spoke this passage from John's Gospel. The vine or stalk is the source of all nutrients. Only shoots which grow directly from it, or have been grafted onto it, bear fruit.

As I look back over my life, I can see that I have produced all sorts of fruit by my *own* effort. What has become a much more important question at this point is: how much of what I produce is the fruit of my relationship with Jesus? In other words, have I allowed myself to become a "daily disciple" of Jesus by being in relationship with Him? Am I grafted onto the vine of Christ?

The bottom line of my experience of *TRUE HEART* is that I am being challenged to open *all* of my heart and my life to God's grace. While the commitment to the Jesuits and the priesthood always felt full-time and lifelong, the *relationship* with Jesus seemed to have an on-again, off-again feel to it. Quite frankly, I was more in control than Christ. Now I feel that I have truly begun to commit to *Jesus*. Twice daily I need to come to Him with my ups and downs, my joys and angers, my loves and victories, my failures and grief, and my *constant* need.

My *constant* need: what does that mean? It means that *TRUE HEART* prayer makes me more aware of my weakness, my failures, and my need for redemption. I have been graced with the eyes to see the reason for Christ's redeeming sacrifice, more clearly than ever before. It is a sacrifice and grace I cannot live without.

Perhaps it is the same discovery of the alcoholic or drug addict. One day, the addict finally wakes up and realizes that the life they thought they controlled is actually out of control.

The only way to salvation is to surrender to love's sobriety and embrace. The alcoholic genuinely in touch with the truth of her/his life knows they are *always recovering* and are never *fully* recovered. One must live constantly with the knowledge of her/his vulnerability and turn to God for help and aid. It is a life of submission, humility, and holy dependence.

Is the invitation to submission, humility and holy dependence the best way for me to convince you to stay committed to *TRUE HEART* prayer? Is this good marketing? Perhaps not, but I am convinced that while your issues may be different from mine, your experience will pull you into the same position of humility, submission, and dependency on God when confronted with the truth of your weakness and need.

What could possibly be attractive about living this way? Praying and living *TRUE HEART* enables a person to be vulnerable, humbly submissive and dependent on God. I can rely on Jesus, who has promised to give me what I need: "If you remain in me and my words remain in you, ask for whatever you want and it will be done for you." (Jn 15: 7)

These words utterly change a person and their world view. Jesus offers this relationship so that my joy "may be full." How so? Because I experience that even in the weakest and most vulnerable condition of my life, Love does not walk away from me. Love has irrevocably committed Himself to me. He sacrificed for me so that I could be whole, and He wants the knowledge of this great love to be known by me on the most intimate level.

He has also promised that this life of discipleship gives great glory to the Father in heaven. Allowing oneself to abide in His love will bear fruit that will give glory to the Father of Jesus Christ. What an awesome reality!

At the beginning of a retreat or in my daily *TRUE HEART* prayer, I try to commit to this relationship. The renewal of my vocational commitment to Christ in the daily engagement with *TRUE HEART* prayer is a means to deepen the knowledge of my radical dependence on God. It fosters the joy of a personal relationship with Christ Jesus that grounds me and opens me up to the deepest yearnings of my heart—my True Heart.

The more I open my heart to a serious relationship with Christ, the more I come to understand the joy for which I have been created. You also have been created for this joy. That is why I am confident you will remain in the embrace of *TRUE HEART* and the Lord Jesus who loves you beyond all reckoning will never let you go. The Love that grounds the universe holds you in His True Heart.

Let us pray for each other that we can all find the joy and peace of living our True Heart!

Peace,

Fr. Bill Watson, S.J.

Sacred Story Press

Seattle, USA

sacredstorypress.com

Sacred Story Press explores dynamic new dimensions of classic Ignatian spirituality, based on St. Ignatius's Conscience Examen in the Sacred Story prayer method, pioneered by Fr. Bill Watson, S.J. We are creating a new class of spiritual resources. Our publications are research-based, authentic to the Catholic Tradition, and designed to help individuals achieve integrated spiritual growth and holiness of life.

We Request Your Feedback

The Sacred Story Institute welcomes feedback on Forty Weeks. Contact us via email or letter (see below). Give us ideas, suggestions, and inspirations for how to make this a better resource for Catholics and Christians of all ages and walks of life. Please also contact us for bulk orders and group discounts.

admin-team@sacredstory.net
Sacred Story Institute & Sacred Story Press
1401 E. Jefferson, Suite 405
Seattle, Washington 98122

TRUE HEART CONNECT
Connect with us on Facebook at
True Heart Biographies

About the Author

Fr. William Watson, S.J., D.Min., has spent over thirty years developing Ignatian programs and retreats. He has collaborated extensively with Fr. Robert Spitzer in the last fifteen years on Ignatian retreats for corporate CEOs. In the spring of 2011, he launched a nonprofit institute to bring Ignatian spirituality to Catholics of all ages and walks of life. The Sacred Story Institute is promoting third-millennium evangelization for the Society of Jesus and the Church by using the time-tested Examination of Conscience of St. Ignatius.

Fr. Watson has served as director of retreat programs at Georgetown University, vice president for mission at Gonzaga University, and provincial assistant for international ministries for the Oregon Province of the Society of Jesus. He holds master's degrees in divinity and in pastoral studies 1986, from Weston Jesuit School of Theology: Cambridge, Mass.). He received his Doctor of Ministry degree in 2009 from The Catholic University of America in Washington, DC.

Made in the USA
Lexington, KY
15 November 2019